SpringerBriefs in Sociology

Series editor

Robert J. Johnson, University of Miami, Coral Gables, FL, USA

More information about this series at http://www.springer.com/series/10410

Bruce K. Friesen

Moral Systems and the Evolution of Human Rights

 Springer

Bruce K. Friesen
University of Tampa
Tampa, FL
USA

ISSN 2212-6368   ISSN 2212-6376   (electronic)
ISBN 978-94-017-9550-0   ISBN 978-94-017-9551-7   (eBook)
DOI 10.1007/978-94-017-9551-7

Library of Congress Control Number: 2014953234

Springer Dordrecht Heidelberg New York London

Printed on acid-free paper

Springer is part of Springer Science+Business Media (www.springer.com)

For Cheryl

Preface

I gasped as I touched the old urn. It was cold to the touch, but surprisingly firm and intact. My gasp was not produced by the urn's temperature but instead from the realization that I had just made contact with a remnant of a shipwreck that changed the course of global history. My students and I were on a tour of the Odyssey Marine Exploration lab in Tampa, Florida, examining some of the cargo of the 400-year-old wreck of the *Buen Jesus y Nuestra Senora del Rosario*. Laden with gold and pearls from the New World, the 1622 sinking of the *Buen Jesus* and other accompanying ships in a surprise storm off the coast of Florida helped to bankrupt the Bank of Madrid. This, in turn, led to the collapse of the Spanish Empire's dominance in the New World. The wreck was discovered in 400 meters (1,312 feet) of water, far too deep for conventional underwater exploration. Exploration was made possible only by using new deep-sea technology created by British engineers to drill for oil in the North Sea.

You're lucky to be alive. Well, I should add, you're lucky to be alive at this particular point in time. New technologies are allowing scientists to produce fascinating discoveries about human beings almost daily, from fields as disparate as archaeology, biology, genetics, neuroscience, anthropology, geology, and even child psychology. Findings from fields such as these are converging to produce a fast-growing, empirically grounded narrative of the emergence of human beings on the planet. It is a remarkable story of survival, endurance, diversity, and adaptation. Though life on earth has existed for millions of years, modern homo sapiens emerged a mere 200,000 years ago in Africa. Other related life forms like Denisovans and Neanderthals evolved prior to and alongside homo sapiens, but eventually died out.

Small groups of homo sapiens began migrating out of Africa roughly 60,000 years ago, likely due to changing climactic conditions. From there, more groups splintered off, taking circuitous routes throughout the globe. Skin lightened as people moved farther away from the equator, an adaptive mechanism that allowed more vitamin D to be absorbed in places where there is less sunlight. Some groups moved east from Africa, along the coast to eventually populate the Indian subcontinent, Southeast Asia, and Australia. Others likely continued across the

Bearing land bridge to eventually inhabit all of North and South America. Though it took thousands of years, it all took place in the blink of an evolutionary eye.

One scientist responsible for drawing public attention to the burgeoning human narrative is National Geographic geneticist Spencer Wells, who shares the human story of global migration with various audiences around the world. As part of the Genographic Project (https://genographic.nationalgeographic.com/), Wells invites people to purchase a DNA collection kit from National Geographic. For a modest sum, the identity-protected DNA samples are analyzed using Y chromosome and mitochondrial DNA markers to identify one's individual genographic history. Genetic markers can be used to trace the likely path of one's ancestors, some of whom migrated out of Africa thousands of years ago and across the globe. Many individuals testify to being deeply moved when reviewing the results of their DNA analysis. Information about one's ancestors is personally meaningful, but the ancestral story which connects us to the stream of human history can be equally powerful. Wells' research, and the technology used to reveal genetic histories, is timely. The pace of global migration is quickening, but most people are familiar only with the recent past of their family history.

The ramifications of this new research for human behavior are only now permeating a few subspecialties of Sociology. Early sociologists such as Marx, Spencer, Durkheim, Tonnies, and others were stimulated to think sociologically as they considered the tumultuous history of human beings and large-scale social change. Sociologists have been particularly fascinated with the transition from traditional to modern societies, but much of the theorizing has typically encompassed larger swaths of human history. Some contemporary theorists like Gerhard Lenski continue the fascination with long-term human social evolution, but today the primary focus remains at the point of industrialization. Few consider the vast pools of knowledge from other disciplines that can inform sociological accounts of the past. Cultural anthropologists and, increasingly, evolutionary biologists are stepping in to fill the void.

Sociology has much to contribute to the ongoing dialogue on human origins. More than other disciplines, Sociology emphasizes the creative and dynamic aspects of human social life over whatever innate or "natural" drives that exist. Social structure; the rules created to govern social life, receives a good deal of attention. Though socially constructed, rules and laws can take on a life of their own and exert great influence on human behavior. "Who benefits?" is the siren song of the sociologist to aid in identifying the unequal ways in which institutions, laws, rules, and customs intentionally or unintentionally privilege some people over others. It is perhaps this careful attention to power dynamics that Sociology has rightly earned the title as the black sheep of the social sciences. Theories from other disciplines like Psychology, Economics, and even Anthropology and Biology, too often end up legitimating the status quo and existing social inequalities. Solid evidence notwithstanding, sociologists suspect that inequalities are most often produced through social rather than natural causes, and focus their analysis on socially constructed mechanisms that produce inequity. Such foci are seldom popular with those who benefit from systems of inequality.

Scientists—both natural and social—need to read each other's work. Potential biases and unstated assumptions in one field can be more easily identified by those working outside of it. Academic work in most Western countries operates in intellectual silos. There are advantages to this system, to be sure. Michèle Lamont's (2010) book, *How Professors Think*, illustrates the drawbacks. Drawing from her years of service on interdisciplinary funding agencies, Lamont notes how too many intellectuals suffer from *homophily*; a tendency to deem as excellent work which closely resembles their own. This applies both to the way in which academics individually practice their own craft as well as the more general epistemological approaches of a particular discipline. Working in academic silos too easily leads one to the erroneous conclusion that their own discipline offers a *full* explanation of human behavior.

Sociologists are generally loath to incorporate findings from the natural sciences into theories of human behavior. Siding heavily with nurture in the nature-nurture debate, sociological approaches begin with the assumption that human beings are more or less born as a *tabula rasa*; a blank slate. This tendency is no doubt motivated by a focus on social processes that make us who we are, but it also emanates from a genuine aversion to theories used in the past to fuel ideological regimes bent on justifying the cruel mistreatment of others. Political regimes *claiming* biological differences between races, sexes, nationalities, social classes, and other categories of human beings have committed heinous acts; most notably during the Holocaust. If these experiences have taught us anything, it is to reject outright theories of biological or neurological difference until a full body of quality information compels us to conclude otherwise.

Scientists are likewise products of their own culture and prone to be influenced by the dominant cultural beliefs of the time. Tavris' (1993) book *The Mismeasure of Woman* provides dozens of illustrations of science done poorly. Finding no meaningful differences between men and women, researchers in Biology, Medicine, and other fields conclude that a methodological error in experimentation must have produced artificial results, rather than considering the potential validity of their own data. Satel and Lilienfeld (2013) note similar problems of interpretation in the current wave of studies in neuroscience. Because the implications of natural science findings are so volatile, consumers would be best served to approach such studies with a healthy dose of *negativistic logic;* assuming no theory to be true until overwhelming evidence to the contrary renders such a position as naive. As the signature line of a colleague's email reads, "Don't stop at an explanation you like."

At the same time, sociological approaches to human behavior would be enhanced by making explicit the naturalistic assumptions included therein. It doesn't take much digging to see that certain biological assumptions are embedded in much sociological work, including that which is constructivist in orientation. Becker's (1953) classic work *Becoming a Marijuana User*, for example, rightly points out how social processes influence the effects of marijuana. At the same time, Becker's work implies that the drug must have *some* type of physiological effect. Otherwise, we could expect similar subcultures to be created around, say, the consumption of paper bags or some other random tangible. What is it about marijuana that motivates groups to create cultures of consumption? Do the effects of the drug in some way frame the manner in which it is consumed or experienced? These qualifications are left unaddressed.

Jack Haas' (1974) research on high-steel ironworkers is another example. Haas describes how social processes are created to essentially test new apprentices to see how they deal with the anxiety produced by the dangers inherent in the occupational work. Implicit in this work is the observation that anxiety *is* a natural response when working in situations where one wrong step could lead to a deadly fall. What kinds of likely behaviors are produced by anxiety? What other features of human chemistry increase or decrease the propensity to feel anxious? How does anxiety influence perception, fatigue, decision-making, or social psychological factors like trust? Biological processes are thus assumed to be antecedent or even intervening in some sociological processes. Making these assumptions explicit could ultimately allow for more sophisticated models of human behavior to be developed by sociologists.

This book is an attempt to synthesize pertinent natural science information in the construction of a sociological theory of morality. It is evident that homo sapiens have evolved over time, that our origins are in Africa, and that we began to colonize the globe roughly 60,000 years ago. Homo sapiens of all shapes, colors, and sizes are of the same family as over 99% of our DNA is identical. Though we today lack more inherent knowledge or "instincts" at birth than other species, a growing body of credible evidence appears to affirm certain behavioral tendencies in humans associated with what we label as morality. What these conditions are, and how they work to inform or provide contingencies for human social behavior, is explained herein. The evidence is consonant with de Waal's (2013:56) assertion that the building blocks of morality are at least a hundred millennia older than current human civilizations and religions.

These findings suggest that religion is a latecomer in the field of morality. If recent global trends continue, religion's influence on issues pertaining to morality in the future may be of limited duration. Despite this, societies with rapidly growing percentages of individuals either non-affiliated with religious organizations or embracing an atheist orientation are not descending into violence and chaos. Every day social life remains ordered, with the vast majority of citizens acting prosocially; respectfully; *morally*. Despite this, researchers like de Waal (2013) and Robbins (2012) fear that science and the naturalistic worldview is inadequate to inspire good behavior as religion does. The position taken throughout this essay is more anthropological. Community life has always been less than idyllic. At the same time, our inner nature, and that of our societal companions, creates a need to construct a moral system which produces more social harmony rather than less. Both past and present societies have created moral systems decoupled from religious beliefs, and have thrived. This observation should offer some comfort to those who fear a descent into chaos as interest in religious orthodoxy and practice continues to wane.

I arrived at an interest in the study of morality in an indirect manner. In receiving an invitation to contribute a book chapter on the globalization of human rights (Friesen 2011), I grappled to explain why human rights emerged when it did, as it did, and in the form it took. As a sociologist, I was fascinated that representatives from many of the world's major religious, philosophical, and cultural traditions came together and created a document about the treatment of other people upon which all could agree. That an emphasis would be placed on equality, given the thousands of years of growing inequality in increasingly complex societies, was indeed puzzling. I found the constructivist accounts of the creation of the Universal Declaration of Human Rights (UHR) far from satisfactory. There were too many repeating themes, too many similarities with the past, to suggest that human rights were the result of a more or less *arbitrary* process of meaning construction. Neither did I find satisfying the accounts of political scientists and others such as Beitz (2011), who suggest that human rights are more about an emergent political practice than an abstract normative idea. That *may* have been true at the outset, but human beings do imbue some aspects of their world with meaning. To suggest otherwise would be to miss the point that the articulation of human rights was simultaneously a creative endeavor *and* a link to our evolutionary and social past. It was a reconnection with our human selves and an incredibly optimistic statement about the future. It had a moral tone, set within a surprisingly inclusive moral framework.

I settled on a sociocultural evolutionary approach to understand the emergence of human rights, but soon found that a theory had not yet been developed to treat the emergence of human rights with the full attention it deserved. Much of the sociological literature regarding morality is subsumed under the rubric of the sociology of religion or the nebulous heading of culture. Neither approach fully accounted for the rise of a secular morality, and using religious nomenclature to refer to such (as in *civil religion*) did more to invoke religion-as-metaphor than it did to explain a unique form of social behavior. In constructing an evolutionary perspective on morality, then, I had to first understand how morality functioned in the role of a community, and the environmental changes that accompanied moral transitions. I have sought to explain why and how it is that moral revolutions occur, and why the concept of human rights has so readily resonated with millions of people. This book thus represents an attempt to fulfill a recommendation of the 2009 NSF Funded *Science of Morality Workshop* to develop more theories that explain morality (Hitlin and Stets 2009: 5).

Chapter 1 outlines the dominant understanding of human sociocultural evolution at this point in time. This provides the context for a discussion of moral evolution. Human beings have organized themselves in increasingly large and complex social entities known as societies. While the history of societies is likewise complex and varying, it is apparent that human societies have evolved over time in the direction of simple to complex, and from small to large. Increasing social inequality too has been a theme, though equally fascinating are the numerous institutionalized mechanisms of redistribution that have attempted to address inequality. In taking a cultural materialist approach, I recognize that these broad changes in social organization *precede* changes in culture, of which morality is a part.

How human societies have managed to create a sense of social unity and collective identity is the subject of Chap. 2. Here I introduce the concept of the moral system and attempt to demonstrate the utility of the concept for understanding social unity and integration. Chapter 3 applies the theory of moral systems to traditional societies in an effort to illustrate the environmental pressures that precipitate a morally adaptive change. Chapter 4 draws on recent natural and social science research on morality. It suggests that the recurring moral themes in human beings are a part of our genetic makeup, having evolved through natural selection to become part of the human condition. These studies aid in understanding feelings of outrage, envy, empathy, or connectedness as a response to social stimuli.

Chapter 5 traces the development of secular morality in the form of a modern nation-state. Nation-states offer the potential of tolerance for diversity, but their collective power and nuclear weaponry have brought about new threats of widespread death and destruction. The chapter goes on to explain how these dangers, realized in the Holocaust and in India's struggle for independence, set in motion the pressures that led to the emergence of human rights. The potential for human rights to serve as a moral system is still being realized. The final chapter engages in social forecasting, describing two possible future scenarios as moral systems continue to evolve. If change is the constant, we can anticipate evolutionary change in moral systems to continue.

A final biographical note: Good ideas are sometimes rejected, not because of the validity of their observations, but because of their implications. I do not mean to imply that the ideas in this volume are necessarily good (though I hope they are), but I am aware that there are times when our own beliefs prevent us from seriously considering the full amount of evidence available. There are times when religious faith enables people to see things clearer, and other times when it inhibits us from seeing all there is to see. Faith is complex. As Marty (1996: 14–15) so keenly observed, "Religion motivates most killing in the world today... Religion contributes to most healing in the world today." Both of these statements are true. Equally telling is how our own assumptions often influence how we receive Marty's two observations. Persons of faith are more likely to downplay or ignore the first, while secularists are more likely to downplay or ignore the second. In reality, *both* statements are true.

In any case, my intent here is *not* to deride or criticize anyone's beliefs, but instead to make an honest attempt to come to terms with the evidence available to us. If it matters to you, I grew up in a religious home and even attended an evangelical Bible college for 4 years. These were some of the best times of my life. I like to believe that I experienced some of the best that religion has to offer. We loved deeply, forgave frequently, and compelled each other to be better people than we were the day before. At the same time, experiences that I had while continuing my college education clearly indicated that some information was being ignored by my religious community. That it took the Catholic Church 350 years to formally apologize for persecuting Galileo for his observation that the earth revolves around the sun is, to me, nothing short of embarrassing. At some point in my education, I realized that truth had to be prioritized before faith. I reasoned that if God was real, God would be revealed in truth. And if not, what business did I have in believing in things that were not true?

One moral lesson I internalized as a kid was the importance of honesty. *Good* science, as a way of knowing, is honest; sometimes brutally so. You have in your hands an honest attempt to induce from the data available at this moment in time a theory of morality. What sense you make of this information, and how you deal with it, is ultimately up to you. We are all on our own journey of discerning truth from falsity. Know that I deeply respect yours.

Tampa, Florida, October 2014   Bruce Friesen

References

Becker, H. S. (1953). Becoming a marihuana user. *The American Journal of Sociology, 59*(3), 235–242.

Beitz, C. (2011). *The Idea of Human Rights*. New York: Oxford University Press.

de Waal, F. (2013). *The Bonobo and the Atheist*. New York: W. W. Norton & Co.

Friesen, B. K. (2011). Globalizing the human rights perspective. In J. Blau & M. Frezzo (Eds.), *Sociology and human rights* (pp. 79–102). Boulder, CO: Paradigm.

Haas, J. (1974). The stages of the high-steel ironworker apprentice career. *The Sociological Quarterly, 15*(4), 93–108.

Hitlin, S., & Stets, J. E. (2009). *NSF report on the science of morality workshop*. Washington, DC: American Sociological Association.

Lamont, M. (2010). *How professors think: Inside the curious world of academic judgment*. Cambridge, MA: Harvard University Press.

Marty, M. (1996). You get to teach and study religion. *Academe, 82*(6), 14–15.

Robbins, R. H. (2012). *Global problems and the culture of capitalism* (5th edn.). Boston, MA: Pearson.

Satel, S., & Lilienfeld, S. O. (2013). *Brainwashed: The seductive appeal of mindless neuroscience*. New York: Basic Books.

Tavris, C. (1993). *The mismeasure of woman*. New York: Touchstone.

Acknowledgments

I am grateful to a number of people and organizations for stimulating my thinking in this area over the years. Friends and colleagues have tolerated my yammering about human rights and have given me additional insight: Jeff Skowronek, James Woodson, Steve Geisz, Marcus Arvan, Ryan Cragun, Susan Brinkley, Doug Marshall, P. Bagavandoss, and Lance Kane have been crucial in this regard. Special thanks go to Scott Husband, who helped me formulate the ideas in Chap. 4, and to longtime friend and special education teacher Jim Penner, for four days of formative dialogue while reading de Waal (2013) together on a houseboat on Lake Cumberland, Kentucky.

Judith Blau invited me to become a part of both *Sociologists Without Borders* (SWB) and the Human Rights Section of the *American Sociology Association*; a section in which I served as Chair in 2011–2012. Keri Iyall Smith, David Brunsma, Judith Blau, Mark Frezzo, Brian Gran, LaDawn Haglund, and Jeong-Woo Koo have provided much support and inspiration. The rich, interdisciplinary dialogue I've experienced as a representative on the *Science and Human Rights Coalition* of the *American Association for the Advancement of Science* (AAAS) motivated me to form a similar interdisciplinary consortium called the *Human Rights Think Tank* at my home University, the University of Tampa. I wouldn't be as far along in my own thinking without input from Margaret Vitullo, Sam McFarland, Jessica Wyndham or other members of these groups. The activities of the Tank have provided increasing contact with the *American Civil Liberties Union*, which formed its own national Human Rights Commission in 2003. Working on real-life issues with Area Director Dr. Joyce Hamilton Henry provides many opportunities for praxis. The University of Tampa provided me with a much appreciated sabbatical in the fall of 2014, during which I was able to complete this manuscript. Both Esther Otten and Hendrikje Tuerlings of Springer Publications have remarkably patient and supportive of this project, and series Editor Robert Johnson has provided quality mentoring well beyond this monograph. They've been a delight to work with.

My wife Cheryl has not only helped to increase the quality of this work, but has provided me with daily inspiration in the way she makes human rights a way of life without even thinking about it. I appreciate the honor of traveling this road with the support of my children, Brittany and Justin, and the hours of dialogue regarding the state of humankind, justice, religion—and motorcycles—with my father and step-mother; Drs. John and Virginia Friesen. My in-laws, Dave and Pat Cronk, and my mother, Ruth Nickel, enrich me daily with their obstinate insistence on being honorable people. Burned in my early memory is the picture of a young housewife and mother of three, standing alone in the hot Kansas sun, loudly chastising two burly police officers for forcibly removing the only two young black girls in a public wading pool. The overcrowded pool had cleared when the black girls entered as a legion of white mothers urgently called their children out. My young sisters and I were delighted to follow our mother's bidding to remain in the empty pool and befriend the little girls. Not much more than five feet tall, my mother towered in stature that day as she modeled for me, in front of all of those condescending mothers, what it means to be a moral person. My attempt to emulate her example has been far from adequate.

Contents

Chapter 1
Introduction

Sociology as Naturalist Inquiry

One wonders what greater theoretical sophistication would be achieved if more sociologists considered themselves naturalists. *Natural history* is the broad and eclectic field of studying organisms in their own environment; those who contribute to the field are called *naturalists*. Collective knowledge, produced in disparate fields by scientists studying isolated species in particular environs, is pooled in the field of natural history. There the totality of information is considered, which produces an ongoing evidence-based narrative of the history of the world and its inhabitants. Enabled with unique ways of knowing wrought by powerful new technologies, corroborating evidence continues to affirm and refine a jaw-dropping grand narrative of human evolutionary history. His epilogue notwithstanding, Kuhn's (1970) accusation that science and its paradigms are not progressive is perhaps better understood as being descriptive of a specific time in the history of science.

Darwin was a naturalist. As a young man he pondered the incredible diversity of species across the world, noting that some species are more common in particular geographic areas than others. In the two decades between his trip to the Galapagos Islands and his publishing of *On the Origins of Species*, Darwin developed the theory of evolution. Environmental change creates the conditions in which various species survive and others do not. In doing so, Darwin demonstrated an openness to consider the long term impact of global forces, including the possibility that aspects of life could be interconnected and intergenerational, and that relationships between environment and biology (i.e. nurture and nature) are inseparable and recursive.

This may have been reasonable, given Darwin's focus and research question. Are these possibilities not equally relevant, though, when considering questions of collective human behavior? Homo sapiens are but one of the earth's millions of

© The Author(s) 2015
B.K. Friesen, *Moral Systems and the Evolution of Human Rights*,
SpringerBriefs in Sociology, DOI 10.1007/978-94-017-9551-7_1

species, having evolved to their current form only within the last 200,000 years. The reality of biological evolution is compelling when the stunning array of evidence is considered. Any discipline that dismisses outright the possibility that evolutionary processes have and continue to shape the human condition closes itself off to an opportunity to more fully explain human behavior. It risks being labeled as naïve and irrelevant. While the natural sciences inform each other, the social sciences; and sociology in particular, have been remarkably resistant to being influenced by other fields which produce additional insights into human behavior. Sociology's preoccupation with the notion of ideology may itself be a function of environmental forces. Sociological theories today are largely produced by individuals living in advanced industrial countries; countries in which intellectuals enjoy a decent standard of living. Lenski (2005: 68) suggests that, having largely met the most critical of biological needs, theorists may be unaware of their importance in predicting human behavior.

Convergence

The last 50 years have seen a veritable explosion of new technologies applied to the naturalist quest to investigate the origins and nature of life on this planet. Some of the most profound developments have been in the fields of information technology, nanotechnology, biotechnology, cognitive science, robotics, and artificial intelligence. Bainbridge and Roco (2005: 2–3) have commented: "Recent advances in nanoscience and nanotechnology enable a rapid convergence of other sciences and technologies for the first time in human history." Because specialized knowledge is needed to use these particular technologies, entirely new subfields have emerged in traditional disciplines. Medicine, for example, has spawned the fields of bioinformatics, synthetic biology, nanobiology, computational biology, tissue engineering, biomaterials, and systems biology—all new interdisciplinary research areas (MIT 2011). Discoveries leading to the mapping of the human genome in 2001 have similarly produced new fields such as paleogenetics; studying the distant past through the preserved genetic remains of ancient organisms, and archaeogenetics; the use of molecular population genetics to study the human past (Renfrew and Boyle 2000).

These new epistemological tools have created enormous opportunities for gathering data on the origins and development of human life on this planet. New technologies have democratized the data gathering process by allowing amateur scientists to access tools that generate new information. Google Earth is but one example. Easy and simple to use, Google Earth allows average citizens the world over to search for and report anomalies in the natural environment that indicate possible human activity (http://www.googleearthanomalies.com/). When investigating the identified anomalies, researchers have found new pyramids and mounds, cave formations containing ancient human skeletons, hidden rain forests, and heretofore undiscovered remains of human civilizations. Radar and microwave imaging from satellites in space can now be used to create powerful images of ruins of civilizations buried under jungles or sand, identifying buried structures to a depth of six feet.

So much new knowledge has been produced by these technologies that one is observing the emergence of a burgeoning new field of what has been called *convergence science* (Berrett 2011). Findings from a variety of fields are considered in their totality in this new endeavor, producing questions, observations, and theories that are greater than the mere sum of their parts. Wilson (1998) used the term *consilience* to refer to a convergence of separate and distinct pieces of evidence affirming a particular conclusion. An example of this type of consilience was expressed in Huxley's (1943) book *Evolution: The Modern Synthesis*. Personally familiar with many scientists and making use of his expansive collection of article reprints, Huxley confirmed the emergent agreement across the natural sciences of the reality of evolution. Widely accepted, the book ushered in a new age of unparalleled growth and discovery under the new paradigm. More recently, Ellis et al. (2013) have suggested a new interdisciplinary approach to study the period of time called the *anthropocene*: the time when homo sapiens came to dominate the globe and make an indelible impact on the biosphere.

In today's terms, no field has been more influential in adding insight to the human family story than the field of genomics. With the mapping of the human genome in 2003, made possible with the assistance of supercomputers, the additional insight into the human story has been unparalleled. Scientists are now able to extract DNA from ancient human remains and track the migrations of humans out of Africa over the past 60,000 years. An entire line of people related to homo sapiens, the Denisovans, was identified using a single fingertip bone. So much new insight into humankind's history has been gleaned through genomics that scientists have attempted to develop a conceptual framework to deal with the increasing cross-pollinization of knowledge, technologies, and paradigms from previously disparate fields. In 2009, the journal *Nature* (2009) published a series of articles attempting to reconcile knowledge from the social sciences and humanities with growing discoveries in the life sciences. Similarly, MIT researchers have identified the coalescing of knowledge in the life sciences, physical sciences, and engineering to be a third revolution in and of itself (the 1953 discovery of the human genome and its 2003 complete sequencing being the first and second, respectively). They note, "convergence does not simply involve a transfer of tool sets from one science to another; fundamentally different conceptual approaches from physical science and engineering are imported into biological research, while life science's understanding of complex evolutionary systems is reciprocally influencing physical science and engineering. Convergence is the result of true intellectual cross-pollination" (MIT 2011: 9).

In recent years, one of the foremost geneticists to both contribute to and popularize the growing implications of genomic research is Spencer Wells. An explorer-in-residence at National Geographic, Wells has created the Genographic Project (https://genographic.nationalgeographic.com/). For a few hundred dollars, any person can painlessly gather a sample of their own DNA via cheek swab and have it analyzed to reveal their own family's deep ancestry. Routes of ancestors who migrated out of Africa can be traced as far back as 60,000 years ago. Though tested anonymously, a person can volunteer to have their results included in a DNA database used to inform the growing picture of ancient human history on this planet. Combined with the genetic samples of specific populations collected by Wells and others, a large, composite picture of human history continues to unfold. When possible, evidence from other fields such as archaeology, anthropology, geology and geography is used to test the validity of genetic analyses. We are the direct beneficiaries of this new information.

The Never-Ending (Back) Story

Two evolutionary histories are relevant for our purposes: the biological evolution of the human species, and the sociocultural evolution of human societies. *Biological evolution* refers to the way in which our species has physically evolved over time, whereas *sociocultural evolution* refers to the changing manner in which human beings have organized themselves in societies. Though distinct in some respects, the two stories heavily influence each other. Biological evolution provides the backstory to our sociocultural evolution, but it does not determine it. Environmental changes can place pressure on species, but not all successfully adapt to the new conditions. Increasingly rapid sociocultural change places ever greater pressure on the human species to physiologically evolve at ever faster rates. In the last 300 years alone, humans have increased in average weight by 50 %, have doubled their longevity, and have improved the functioning of vital organ systems (Kotler 2013). The relationship between biology and environment is best approached as an interplay, or dialogue, between the two systems. This interplay is critical when considering the evolution of morality and moral systems over time.

Equally important to consider is the very short time of evolutionary history in which human beings have inhabited the earth. It is informative to note that the vast majority of the earth's 4.5 billion years of history have included no human beings. *Hominids*—that is, early ancestors of human beings—separated from modern apes a mere 5–8 million years ago. Since that time, at least a dozen different humanlike species evolved; only some of which are direct descendants of homo sapiens. We know this as new fossil discoveries, such as the Red Deer Cave people found in 2012 (Barras 2012), show evidence of genetically unique strands of hominids. All of these branches eventually died out, with the exception of homo sapiens. There is evidence, though, that at least two of these branches; Neanderthals and Denisovans, mated with homo sapiens (Zimmer 2013; Harmon 2012).

Modern homo sapiens evolved to their current form roughly 200,000 years ago. Earliest fossils of humans date to this period, and are found at Omo Kibish in Ethiopia. Two hundred thousand years sounds like a long period of time, though 200,000 years is a mere hiccup of time in the span of 4.5 billion years. By contrast, dinosaurs roamed the earth for 135 million years before succumbing to extinction. Of the 200,000 years of "modern" human history, humans lived exclusively in Africa until as recently as 50,000 BCE, when changing climactic conditions drew some migrants out of the continent and into the Middle East. From there, humans eventually went on to populate the entire earth. Wells (2004) details the fantastical story of the human diaspora in his book, *The Journey of Man: A Genetic Odyssey*. Genetic analysis, corroborated by geologic, anthropological, archaeological, and geographic information, has made possible the telling of this story in detail never before experienced. Close to extinction about 60,000 years ago, homo sapiens recovered and eventually went on to migrate out of Africa. Some bands of humans went on to populate India and Australia around 40,000 years ago. Additional waves of migration populated the Middle East. Throughout the generations, some continued north, and then branched either west into Europe or east into Asia. Homo sapiens began appearing in the Americas about 20,000 years ago. Though still somewhat contested (Deloria 1997), a dominant theory suggests a group from Asia traversed the Bering land bridge and began to populate the continent of North America. Six thousand years later, their descendants reached the southernmost point of South America.

As people migrated, their physical features began to change as they adapted to new environmental conditions. The skin lightened among those who moved away from the equator, helping to absorb more vitamin D from the sun. Other physical features may have grown prominent because of its perceived attractiveness or simply inherited dominance, such as the epicanthic eye trait among many peoples in Asia. Homo sapiens continued to reproduce as they migrated. By year 0, the global population had reached 300,000 from a mere 10,000 in 60,000 BCE. By 1800 AD, the world's population had reached 1 million. It would take another 1,800 years for the global population to reach 1 billion. Since then, the world's population has mushroomed to over 7 billion inhabitants today; more than doubling in size in the last 50 years alone. Note here the incredible amount of change, growth, and development in a remarkably brief period of the earth's history. Change is the constant when describing the evolutionary history of humankind.

The Evolution of Human Societies

The history of modern homo sapiens is inextricably linked with *collective* survival. Since their arrival, humans have preferred banding together in groups as opposed to isolated individual existence. Though group size has greatly expanded in the last few thousand years, the human tendency to live collectively is an organic part of our composition. This is important, as any political, moral, or social philosophy needs to take into account the interdependent and social nature of humankind. Even philosophies embracing or respecting the presumed autonomy of the individual person assume a modicum of social contact and organization.

Lenski (1984) has presented a typology of societies useful for conceptualizing the major socioevolutionary changes in human living conditions over time.

After emerging in their modern form, all human beings lived in small *hunting and gathering societies*. As recently as 12,000 years ago, some of these communities transitioned to *simple horticultural societies*. Herding and fishing societies were variants of this type of transition, depending on the geographic area and available resources. As horticultural societies banded together, large scale *agrarian societies* began to emerge some 5,500 years ago. These included maritime societies in areas situated along coastlines. Though precursors of industrialism appeared in different areas of the world prior to the late 19th century, developed *industrial societies* began to emerge in Western Europe by the 1800s. Though not identified by Lenski and somewhat contested, other authors have suggested the emergence of a *post-industrial society* (Bell 1976) which focuses on the control of information and services as opposed to the mechanization so dominant in industrial society.

Before each of these societal types are described, it is worth making qualifying observations. First, it would be erroneous to assume that these stages of sociocultural transition necessarily imply *progress* of some kind. Progress is a value-laden word with elitist implications. Whether or not progress has occurred is highly dependent upon the criteria selected to assess progress. It *is* true that change has occurred. Advanced agrarian and industrial societies are generally more populous and make use of more complex technologies than hunting and gathering or horticultural societies. Is this necessarily progress? Those living in technologically advanced societies are often eager to label their way of life as superior to earlier ways of life. This implies, of course, that the millions of people who live in societies that have not followed this evolutionary path are in some way delayed, deficient, or backward. Such an approach belies a perceptive bias known as *ethnocentrism*; a tendency to assume that one's own way of life is superior to all others. Much of the death, suffering, and hardship wrought by global colonialism can be attributed to ethnocentric attitudes.

Second, though an overall pattern of change from the technologically simple to complex can be observed, it is equally important to recognize the exceptions. Social change, even evolutionary change, is rarely linear. Western Europe, for example, spent centuries living in the shadow of a larger and more complex society known as the Roman Empire. Those years were called the Dark Ages; a time when social and technological complexity reverted back to simple horticultural style economies. Sociocultural change is also uneven. The Mayans of Central America developed one of the world's greatest civilizations around 1000 BC. They built magnificent temples while most Europeans lived as nomadic barbarians, and organized tens of thousands of people in a society stretching from Mexico to Costa Rica, long before Greece and Rome hit their stride. With the development of global culture, many societies today are attempting to transition directly from simple horticultural or agrarian economies to industrialized societies. Nolan and Lenski (2011) call these *hybrid societies*.

Finally, most social change theorists today reject the overt determinism incumbent in earlier accounts of sociocultural evolution, replacing them with more sophisticated probabilistic models. Deterministic explanations posit that, given a certain condition, a given result will *always* occur. Modern theorists identify independent variables that can exert pressure on societies to change, but predict *likely*, as opposed to *certain* outcomes. Probabilistic models allow for the role of human agency and other factors to produce outcomes different than what might otherwise be expected. Probabilistic explanations offer a better account for the considerable nonlinear patterns of development of societies, including their own potential demise.

Bellah (2011) describes the evolutionary process as the development of *new capacities*; a gradual accumulation of small improvements which better fit a species for its environment and thus increase chances of survival. Capacities no longer useful may be retained, at least until they are lost or modified by new adaptations. Some experts hypothesize that humans were fish at one time in our deep evolutionary past. Most of the biological capacities to exist as fish have been lost, but some physical features remain. These may include the philtrum, or lip groove immediately beneath the nose (Mosley 2011). Bellah applies the concept of new capacities mostly to our biological evolution, but includes in the concept the evolution of innate behavioral tendencies like the capacity for empathy and the universality of parental care. Innate behavioral tendencies have clear implications for understanding sociocultural evolution, as they can both create the potential for the development of new cultural forms and set limits on what is likely to emerge. Though insightful, new capacities alone cannot explain the different rates of sociocultural evolution across societies. Dozens of hunter-gatherer societies still exist in many places, including the central rain forest, south-western desert regions in Africa and the Middle East, arid and semi-arid regions of Australia, and the Arctic. Any theory of socioevolutionary change must therefore account for the fact that evolutionary processes have not had the same degree of impact on all human societies.

Lenski's Taxonomy

Lenski's (1984) taxonomy of the evolution of human societies remains popular within Sociology. The stages of sociocultural evolution are marked by revolutionary changes in the economy. An *economy* is a social arrangement regarding how people in a society collectively survive. Thus, the economy of a hunting and gathering society is primarily the activities of hunting for game and gathering other foodstuffs like berries, roots, and other edibles. Two features of economic life are common to all societies: a division of labor, and mechanisms of redistribution. The former refers to the way work is divided among members of the society, while the latter refers to the sharing of provisions and services so that the lives of all are sustained. Though redistributive mechanisms vary greatly across societies, they are usually based upon principles of compassion and reciprocity. The first principle seeks to reduce the suffering of others, while the latter invokes a sense of responsibility to act in kind if the tables were turned. Respect for such principles also appears to be rooted within the human condition; a point demonstrated in Chap. 4.

Hunting and Gathering Societies

Modern humans have lived in hunter-gatherer societies for 190,000 of their 200,000 year history. Some human beings continue to live in hunting-gathering style societies even today, though their numbers are in steep decline. Similar in some ways to the size and structure of great ape societies (chimpanzees, bonobos, gorillas, and orangutans), humans in hunter-gatherer societies have existed in small roaming *bands* of 25–50 individuals subdivided into clans or families. Though economically autonomous, individual bands are often affiliated with a larger cultural unit called a *tribe*. Tribes share a similar culture and language and are often connected through ties of intermarriage. Periodic gatherings of bands of the same tribe are common, consisting of days of celebration, gift-giving, marriage, and political alignments. Siksika Indians of the Blackfoot Confederacy of the Canadian Northwest, for example, have been gathering for many years in a valley known as the Blackfoot Crossing near Gleichen, Alberta. The site was used for the signing of Treaty #7 in 1877 (http://www.blackfootcrossing.ca/).

Despite the considerable diversity in cultures, location, geography, diet, and history, hunting and gathering societies share a number of common features. Their size rarely exceeds 50 people. Age and gender are used almost universally as the basis for a division of labor, though societies may assign duties differently to men and women or the young and the aged. Life is typically nomadic as the band moves on once an area's resources are depleted. High mortality rates before age 15 keep the average lifespan relatively short, but those who survive past age 15 have an average lifespan of 72 years in contemporary hunter-gatherer societies (Gurven and Kaplan 2007).

Respect for the aged is high since older members of the band are the repositories of accumulated wisdom. Their life experiences and lessons learned from their own elders comprise the knowledge needed for the group's survival. It is thus no surprise that *ancestor worship*; the belief that the spirit of an ancestor continues to exist after death, is a component of religious activities in many hunting and gathering societies. Most groups also subscribe to a type of belief system known as *animism*; the attribution of human-like consciousness to non-human objects or phenomena. In other words, animism is a belief in non-human souls (Tylor 1871). Attribution of a soul is made to animals, wells, mountains, and other aspects of existence important to the group. Many experts refrain from referring to animism as a religion, as its characteristics are qualitatively different than those typically associated with an organized belief system. Most expressions of animism do not include deities, and the diversity of beliefs across animistic tribes belies any attempt at categorization. Animistic beliefs among hunter-gatherers has been widespread.

Because hunter-gatherers were nomadic, people owned few resources. Sharing and redistribution practices were widespread and often embedded in community rituals. The political nature of hunter-gatherers was egalitarian, with little differentiation made by way of status or power. Many tribes existed without a leader or "chief," engaging instead in collective decision-making. The way of life of hunter-gatherers seriously challenges many of the popular assumptions of humans as necessarily competitive and hierarchical, or in need of someone to serve as a leader.

Climate, technology and other resources allowed some hunting and gathering communities to increase in number in some places. These became the likely forerunners of horticultural and pastoral societies. Star Carr in North Yorkshire, England, shows evidence of permanent residence as early as 8770 BC, while Howick House in Northumberland, England, dates to 7600 BCE. Substantial postholes on these sites imply large structures, indicating that hunter-gatherers established permanent settlements when fish and game were plentiful. One of the most fascinating recent finds is Gobekli Tepe; an expansive site in southeastern Turkey. Consisting of finely carved limestone pillars estimated to weigh 10–15 tons apiece, Gobekli Tepe appears to have been used primarily as worship space by hunter-gatherers. No evidence of people residing at the site has been found. Carbon dating places construction of the site somewhere between 12,000 and 10,000 BCE. Recent research has uncovered other complex archaic sites, including Dwarka; under water today off the west coast of India, and Gunung Padang in Indonesia. These finds continue to inform the study of sociocultural evolution.

Simple Horticultural and Pastoral Societies

Hunters and gatherers likely knew for thousands of years how plants and animals could be domesticated. It has only been comparatively recently in human history, however, that some communities transitioned to an economy built on planting and harvesting, or tending to and slaughtering domesticated livestock. New discoveries, like those mentioned above, make it difficult to pinpoint the earliest of these civilizations, but the generally accepted date is 10,000 BCE. The first horticultural societies appeared in what has come to be known as the "fertile crescent" or Mesopotamia, depicted in Fig. 1.1. It is located between two parallel rivers, the Tigris and Euphrates; a 640 mile strip of land located in today's Iraq. Nolan and Lenski (2011) suggest changing climatic conditions and increasing populations likely forced some hunter-gatherers to innovate technologically and culturally so as to sustain their people. Fascinating to note, though, is the independent emergence of horticultural and pastoral societies in various places of the world. Evidence has been collected of domesticated cattle more than 10,000 years ago in China (University of York 2013). Farming activities developed 9,000 years ago in China and Southeast Asia. By 6,000–7,000 BCE parts of Africa, Mesoamerica, and North America were engaged in similar activities.

Shifting from hunting and gathering to raising crops and animals had implications for many facets of society. People transitioned from a nomadic to a sedentary lifestyle. Villages emerged and social life became more formalized and increasingly hierarchical. Food surpluses were produced because food was more plentiful, while health and longevity increased apace. New technologies of food storage

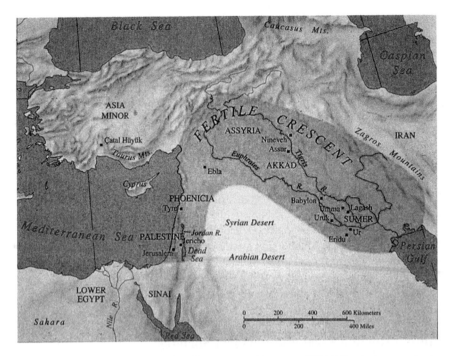

Fig. 1.1 Map of the fertile crescent. http://www.vector-clip-art.com/2011/06/ancient-mesopotamia-map-062611.html

were invented, and social inequality emerged as some people were able to produce more surplus than others. Villages fortified themselves to protect against plundering by outside groups. Village chiefs emerged and, as other villages were either taken over or aligned through intermarriage, the size of social units continued to grow. In early horticultural societies chiefs often played the role of servant, not leader, of their people. People would give gifts to the chief, with the expectation that the chief would distribute any excess to tribal members in need of assistance. Mauss (1912/1990) long ago documented the widespread function of gift-giving as a mechanism to induce goodwill and reciprocity, both within and across archaic societies.

As societies grew, however, social and economic inequality became more common. Chiefs, religious leaders, and more wealthy families were able to remove themselves from the daily drudgery of engaging in work that sustains their own lives by hiring or enslaving other people to do it for them. While this further entrenched social inequality, it also freed a class of people from time-consuming work. In turn, social elites took more time to ponder and think, leading to the development of art, aesthetics, philosophy, and the formalization of religion. As they transitioned, many societies shifted their focus from animism to polytheism; a belief in the existence of multiple gods. This likely evolved as increasing power and awareness was attributed to some animistic spirits.

Advanced Agrarian Societies

Until recently, archaeologists believed that the development of advanced agrarian societies didn't develop much before 3500 BCE. Recent information and discoveries, like Gobekli Tepe, Dwarka, and Gunung Padang may push this date back even farther. Geopolitics and violent conflicts have severely curtailed the ability to further investigate promising archaeological sites in many parts of the world. Iraqi Kurdistan alone has more than 3,000 heritage sites within its borders. Ninety-eight percent of them have not been examined, while a re-examination of previously excavated sites using new instruments could also reveal many new insights (Bradshaw 2013). Ur, the city of the Biblical Abraham, gave up an estimated ten percent of its treasures when last excavated in the 1930s. Most recently, the ruins have been used by both Iraqis and Americans as part of a military base (Clement 2011).

Characterized by ownership of large tracts of land which include big cities and towns, agrarian societies arose as centralized coordination between tribes and villages developed. Over time, agrarian societies came to sustain the lives of thousands of inhabitants. The development of the plow and the use of irrigation techniques facilitated the large-scale growth of crops, capable of feeding thousands. Known also as *classical civilizations*, these societies included towns and cities, monumental architecture, craft specialization, occupational differentiation, and writing and record keeping. Extreme social and economic inequalities were realized as people were organized into social *strata* including slaves, free laborers, nobles and military leaders, and royalty. Opportunities differed greatly by the strata into which one was born. Mobility between strata was virtually nonexistent. A corresponding religious trend in agrarian societies was the rise of monotheism, or belief in a single, all-powerful deity. Emperors or kings of agrarian societies commonly identified themselves as gods or, at least, the one person to receive special dispensations. Extravagant religious temples and sites were constructed, and a full-time clergy emerged to handle religious matters.

Precursors of agrarian societies emerged first in Mesopotamia around 4500 BCE, followed closely by the Harrappan civilization of Northern India. By 3500 BCE, these places had developed into advanced agrarian societies. Classic Egyptian civilization emerged by 3100 BCE. Classical Greek civilization developed by 2700 BCE, though experts suspect its precursors might have appeared as early as 4000 BCE. Far away from these areas, China's classic civilization was established by 3800 BCE, Africa's Land of Punt civilization in Ethiopia by 2500 BCE, and the Americas' Olmec civilization by 1500 BCE. Aspects of the mound builder society of the Mississippi delta emerged around 500 CE. These are but some examples.

Though categorizing agrarian societies into a similar conceptual category can be advantageous, it is important to also keep in mind their unique cultures, histories, and trajectories. Some civilizations emerged on the scene much earlier than others. Some were longer-lasting. On the Yucatan peninsula of Latin America, for example, new research has established Mayan civilization flourishing by 1000 BCE (Inomata et al. 2013). Though in decline since 900 AD, Mayan kings continued their rule until they were exterminated by the Spanish at the dawn of the 18th century. Mayan rule thus extended for a period spanning almost 3,000 years. By contrast, the United States is not yet 250 years old. When most Europeans lived as nomadic barbarians and Greeks lived in small city states, the Maya organized tens of thousands of people into sophisticated societies replete with nobles, priests, merchants, and warriors. The Mayan civilization stretched from Mexico to Costa Rica when the Roman Empire had yet to be conceived. Though the Maya did not invent writing or epigraphy, they greatly enhanced their use and sophistication. Such observations challenge ever-popular but simplistic unilinear theories of sociocultural development.

Industrial Societies

Technological innovation has played an ever-increasingly role in sociocultural change. Digging sticks and domesticated plants and animals facilitated the transition to horticultural societies, while irrigation and the plow fostered agrarian civilizations capable of sustaining the lives of thousands. The advent of industrialization saw a concerted focus on *mechanizing* labor previously performed by human beings. Applying machine technology to tasks raised the importance of science and engineering. It brought people together in a new social invention called the factory, where people and machines worked in concert.

Implications for social and economic life in industrial society have been enormous. Bell (1976) successfully predicted the implosion of the Soviet Union, arguing that the logic of industrialism was incompatible with a political system based on communism. In the West, industrialization closely followed the formation of a new invention called the nation-state; delineated by clearly defined national borders, a strong central government and a national military. Because people encompassed within nation-states were diverse, displaying a use of regional languages, religions, foods, and identities, governments embarked on aggressive programs to cultivate cultural homogeneity and a national identity. This included the adoption of a dominant language and, often, a national religion. A system of mass schooling was eventually implemented to facilitate these changes. Patriotism to the new state was developed through pledges of allegiance, national anthems, and history classes taught with a positive slant towards the nation-state and its leaders. Required military service was used in similar ways.

Robbins (2012) describes how peoples' lives were further altered by the transition from agrarian lifestyles to those centered around factory-based work. Slave and serf castes were transformed over time to the new *labor* class. To ensure income for the state, citizens became *consumers* and national and local taxes were implemented. Owners of factories came to see themselves as *capitalists*, legally required through their corporate charters to act selfishly in the pursuit of profit for profit's sake. In some ways these changes brought improvements to the quality of life for many. Extreme poverty declined, while both health and longevity improved. Opportunities for advancement were opened for far larger proportions of the population than prior to industrialization. Some dangerous or monotonous manual labor tasks were eventually replaced by machines, freeing people to pursue more fulfilling avenues of work. Nationalized social programs saw the emergence of a middle class style of life for many.

Challenges also accompanied the growth of industrial society. Members of the new labor class found themselves increasingly dependent upon factors outside of their control for survival, such as provision of employment, a livable wage, job security and benefits, opportunities for advancement, and jobs available locally so workers could stay connected to their families, community, and place of identity. These have not always been forthcoming. Though economic inequality generally declined from that experienced in agrarian societies, most advanced industrialized countries have experienced a gross concentration of wealth among a very small percentage of the population and a shrinking of the middle class in the last 30 years. The advent of global capitalism has created a very wealthy and powerful small elite, while multinational corporations have been able to manipulate political processes for their own purposes. Pollution concerns need to be addressed on a global scale, while the increasing frequency and severity of economic crises has created uncertainty and economic instability for many families. The technology, knowledge, and tools are there to deal with many of these issues, but clarity and political will is too often lacking.

Advanced industrial societies continue to evolve. Work is increasingly specialized. The proportion of jobs available in service industries has mushroomed while jobs in extractive (e.g. mining, forestry, fishing, farming) and manufacturing industries has declined. The importance of information technologies like cell phones and the internet have greatly altered the ways in which human beings connect and communicate. At the same time, new social forms have emerged whose power transcends those of the nation-state. The annual income of a single multinational company is greater than the combined gross national product of most developing nations. The United Nations (UN), North Atlantic Treaty Organization (NATO), the World Bank, International Monetary Fund (IMF), and other international organizations continue to influence the behavior of nation-states without democratic representation.

Some theorists suggest that the invention of the microchip is facilitating the emergence of a new form of "post-industrial" society, though others remain skeptical. Urry (2000) suggests that the modern world is better understood as *flows* of information, capital, and people, as the notion of a static nation-state has been surpassed. Whether these forces lead to the development of new social forms remains to be seen.

A number of observations can be taken away from this brief review. Human beings are but one of many species that have existed on earth, and our time here has been comparatively brief and quite recent. Sociocultural change has occurred in the last 12,000 years, but the *rate* of change since the advent of industrialization has been exponential. Sociocultural evolution has been uneven and nonlinear, though overall trends toward increasing technological sophistication and population size has been observed. Sociologists identify industrialization as a watershed moment in human history; providing a serious break with the traditional societies of the past. Societies prior to industrialization were predicated upon a desire to maintain static social structures and inhibit change, whereas change is more the constant in modern life.

For our purposes, it is important to consider the substantial amount of diversity of religious belief systems over the past 200,000 years and to note how the growth of polytheism and monotheism generally accompanied societal shifts to horticultural and agrarian societies respectively. Sociocultural changes appear to influence both religious belief and religious expression. Almost all of the world's major religions emerged only after the transition to agrarian ways of life. Each of these religions began as a cult; juxtaposed in belief and practices to the traditions of the dominant society. Judaism, one of the world's oldest continuously practiced major religions, is barely 3,800 years old. Yet despite the incredible diversity of religious thought and expression, human beings have continued to live together and develop prescriptions for living that encourage prosocial behavior, also known as moral behavior. Morality has, can, and does exist apart from religion, though the coupling of religion and morality has varied greatly throughout human history.

I will attempt to illustrate in this book why an incursion into the study of morality will be a more fruitful endeavor to understanding human societies and human behavior than will the study of religion per se. Evidence will be presented to indicate that all moral systems are ultimately informed by an innate and archaic neural architecture in homo sapiens which produces predictable emotional responses to *social* situations. The fact that these emotions are produced only through social interaction renders them irreducibly social in nature. Social factors like history, context, politics, economic systems, and group size heavily influence the particular expression of a moral system, but their root origins are tribal; having evolved over time to become part of what I prefer to call our neuro-sociological nature.

Humans living in groups recognize our interdependent nature by constructing moral systems which attempt to integrate societal members and regulate those situations which typically induce emotional states which can threaten the cohesion, and thus the survival, of the collective. Embedded in all moral systems are calls for group members to practice prosocial behaviors such as empathy, compassion, and consolation. Given a profound aversion to inequality, moral systems embed notions of fairness and reciprocity into moral codes. Because negative visceral reactions to inequality are most easily induced at the micro level, behaviors which reduce inequality, especially at the face-to-face level, are seen as virtuous. Moral systems encourage us to control our anti-social tendencies, but they cannot prevent such emotions from being produced.

Religious belief systems develop as a way to reinforce the importance of a group's moral system and often raise the stakes for noncompliance with the threat of ethereal or eternal consequences. Religion, though, is more often a consequence than cause of a group's morals. All religions are types of moral systems, but all moral systems do not take the form of religion. Religions make truth claims regarding the essential, immutable, and unchanging nature of things. At the same time, substantial change in belief, rituals, and worship continues to occur over time. This is because the social component of moral systems; that which is collectively constructed, is forced to evolve as groups evolve. A focus on morality as distinct from religion can thus help explain the vast diversity of religious expressions over time while acknowledging their common goals. Such an approach may even assist us in developing more flexible, dynamic, and adaptive moral systems in the future. In modernity, abstract secular moral systems increasingly replace the static religious moral systems of the past. How this happens is the subject of this book.

References

Bainbridge, W. S., & Roco, M. C. (2005). *Managing Nano –Bio –Info -Cogno Innovations*. The Netherlands: Springer.

Barras, C. (2012, March). Chinese human fossils unlike any known species. *New Scientist*. http://www.newscientist.com/article/dn21586-chinese-human-fossils-unlike-any-known-species.html#.UkHiGtIqhng. Accessed 24 September 2013.

Bell, D. (1976). *The coming of post-industrial society*. New York: Basic Books.

Bellah, R. (2011). *Religion in human evolution: From the paleolithic to the axial age*. Cambridge, MA: Harvard University Press.

Berrett, D. (2011, January 5). The rise of 'convergence' science. *Inside higher ed*. http://www.insidehighered.com/news/2011/01/05/is_convergence_the_new_big_idea_for_health_sciences. Accessed 10 September 2013.

Bradshaw, R. (2013). Travels to Mesopotamia. *Current World Archaeology, 6*(1), 52–55.

Clement, J. (2011, June 20). Iraq's ancient Ur site in danger. *Discovery.com*. http://news.discovery.com/history/archaeology/ur-archaeological-site-iraq-110620.htm. Accessed 13 December 2013.

Deloria, V. (1997). *Red earth, white lies*. Golden, CO: Fulcrum Pub.

Ellis, E., Fuller, D., Kaplan, J., & Lutters, W. (2013, December 3). Dating the anthropocene: Towards an empirical global history of human transformation of the terrestrial biosphere. *Elementa*. doi:10.12952/journal.elementa.000018. www.elementascience.org. Accessed 7 December 2013.

Gurven, M., & Kaplan, H. (2007). Longevity among hunter-gatherers: A cross-cultural comparison. *Population and Development Review, 33*(2), 321–365. http://www.anth.ucsb.edu/faculty/gurven/papers/GurvenKaplan2007pdr.pdf.

Harmon, K. (2012, August 30). New DNA analysis shows ancient humans interbred with Denisovans. *Scientific American*. http://www.scientificamerican.com/article.cfm?id=denisovan-genome. Accessed 24 September 2013.

Huxley, J. (1943). *Evolution: The modern synthesis*. New York: Harper and Brothers.

Inomata, T., Triadan, D., Aoyama, K., Castillo, V., & Yonenobu, H. (2013). Early ceremonial constructions at Ceibal, Guatemala, and the origins of Lowland Maya civilization. *Science, 340*(6131), 467–471. doi:10.1126/science.1234493.

Kotler, S. (2013, March). Evolution's next stage. *Discover*. http://discovermagazine.com/2013/march/13-evolution-full-tilt#.UkH2ldIqhng. Accessed 24 September 2013.

Kuhn, T. (1970). *The structure of scientific revolutions*. Chicago, IL: University of Chicago Press.

Lenski, G. (1984). *Power and privilege*. Chapel Hill: UNC Press.

Lenski, G. (2005). *Ecological-evolutionary theory*. Boulder, CO: Paradigm.

Mauss, M. (1912/1990). *The gift*. London: Routledge.

MIT. (2011). *The third revolution: The convergence of the life sciences, physical sciences, and engineering*. Washington, DC: MIT Washington Office. http://dc.mit.edu/sites/dc.mit.edu/files/MIT%20White%20Paper%20on%20Convergence.pdf. Accessed 10 September 2013.

Mosley, M. (2011, May 5). Anatomical clues to human evolution from fish. *BBC News*. http://www.bbc.co.uk/news/health-13278255. Accessed 8 October 2013.

Nature. (2009). Science and society series on convergence research. *EMBO Reports*. http://www.nature.com/embor/focus/convergence_research/index.html. Accessed 12 September 2013.

Nolan, P., & Lenski, G. (2011). *Human societies* (11th ed.). Boulder, CO: Paradigm.

Renfrew, C., & Boyle, K. (Eds.). (2000). *Archaeogenetics: DNA and the population prehistory of Europe*. Cambridge: McDonald Institute for Archaeological Research.

Robbins, R. (2012). *Global problems and the culture of capitalism* (5th ed.). Boston, MA: Pearson.

Tylor, E. (1871). *Primitive culture*. London: John Murray.

University of York. (2013, November 8). Origins of cattle farming uncovered in China. *Past Horizons*. http://www.pasthorizonspr.com/index.php/archives/11/2013/origins-cattle-farming-uncovered-china. Accessed 24 November 2013.

Urry, J. (2000). *Sociology beyond societies*. New York: Routledge.

Wells, S. (2004). *The journey of man: A genetic odyssey*. New York: Random House.

Wilson, E. (1998). *Consilience: The unity of knowledge*. New York: Knopf.

Zimmer, C. (2013, March 4). Interbreeding with neanderthals. *Discover*. http://discovermagazine.com/2013/march/14interbreeding-neanderthals#.UkHmrdIqhni. Accessed 24 September 2013.

Chapter 2
The Moral System

The ultimate goal of this monograph is to explain the emergence of human rights as homo sapiens' first truly indigenous global moral system. In order to do so we must first identify and describe the component of society most relevant to the discussion, and then explain how and why it evolves. This chapter describes the concept of the moral system, illustrating ways in which it is related to, but distinct from, the notion of religion. The notion of a moral system is used as a conceptual tool to assist in the analysis and understanding of rapid-paced changes in beliefs over time. Once defined, a theory of how moral systems change will be elucidated and propositions of the theory will be clarified. Subsequent chapters will apply the theory to traditional and modern societies respectively, in an effort to illustrate how moral systems evolve.

Secularizing Durkheim: Key Concepts

Durkheim (1912/1962) attempted to create a science of morality within Sociology that would objectively analyze and explain how it is that moral systems develop and function in societies at large. Early in his career, Durkheim had largely dismissed religion as a relic of traditional societies and predicted its eventual demise and replacement with a new norm he called the *cult of the individual*. Noting religion's durability, Durkheim returned to examine its function later in life. He defined it as, "…a unified system of beliefs and practices relative to sacred things, that is to say, things set apart and forbidden-beliefs and practices which unite in one single moral community called a Church, all those who adhere to them" (1912/1962: 44). Durkheim rightly viewed religion as *sui generis*, but came to view its role in social integration as essential in many ways.

© The Author(s) 2015
B.K. Friesen, *Moral Systems and the Evolution of Human Rights*,
SpringerBriefs in Sociology, DOI 10.1007/978-94-017-9551-7_2

It is unfortunate in my mind that Durkheim returned to focus on religion as the basis of morality, as recent global trends in the rise of non-belief and the development of secular moral systems indicate that Durkheim's initial prognostication may have been prescient. While prejudice against non-believers abounds (Cragun et al. 2012), it is clear that they possess moral commitments in spite of their non-belief. If a definition of morality includes a sense of respect for others, it is clear that non-believers are moral human beings (Cragun 2013; Didyoung et al. 2013). Durkheim's preoccupation with religion, then, may have inhibited his efforts to develop a true science of morality.

Other research that makes use of religious terms, metaphors, rituals, and processes as *explanation* similarly obfuscates more than it clarifies. The study of religion is clearly a worthwhile endeavor in its own right. Yet *if* religion's primary function is embedded in something other than, or in addition to, a religious reality, inquiry is best served if the analytical concepts and terms used actually clarify rather than confuse or befuddle. At times it appears that religious terms are intentionally used to infer a greater religious reality than might otherwise exist. This includes the use of religious jargon or definitions used to refer to ubiquitous human qualities. The redefinition of humanistic values as "spirituality," is but one example of this slight-of-hand (Cragun and Kosmin 2013). It does more to artificially inflate the proportion of respondents identified as religious than it does to document genuine changes in values and the rise of new moral movements. When national and international data clearly show a persistent decrease in religious activity and an incumbent increase in people identifying themselves as having no religious affiliation or as atheist (PEW 2012a, b), describing the current religious climate as *post-secular* (Habermas 2008) seems disingenuous.

By shifting the focus from religion to morality, then, we can more clearly identify moral activity regardless of its religious or non-religious manifestations. To do this, I choose to "secularize" some of Durkheim's key concepts (Friesen 2013) by replacing terms normally associated with religion to something more benign. In particular, I wish to modify Durkheim's useful sacred/profane dichotomy. Drawing on the observations made by himself and his nephew Marcel Mauss in *Primitive Classification* (Durkheim and Mauss 1963), Durkheim argued in *Elementary Forms of the Religious Life* (1912/1962) that religions divide the world into two realms: the *sacred* and the *profane*. Components of the sacred involve those aspects normally associated with religion, while profane aspects of life are those which are outside the religious realm. Typically mundane aspects of life most often comprise elements of the profane, such as getting dressed or cleaning up after a meal. Profane activities and symbols are viewed neither as moral nor immoral; but *amoral*; having no religious significance.

Modifying these concepts to focus exclusively on morality and moral behavior is not difficult. As Hume (1739/1985) long ago noted, moralizing; the dividing of the world into favorable (good) and unfavorable (bad) elements, is a quintessential human behavior. People who come together to form a community likewise construct a weltanschauung, or world view. Moralizing is an essential feature of every weltanschauung. Certain aspects of existence are attributed *moral* meaning; either good or bad. I'll call this the *moral realm*. The remainder of collective experience is part of what I will refer to as the *amoral realm*. Neither good nor bad, aspects of existence within the amoral realm are morally benign. A third potentially useful concept is what can be called the *nonmoral* realm. Aspects of life not yet encountered, that have yet to be cognitively processed by the community in order to designate it as part of the moral or amoral realm, would be part of the nonmoral realm. For example, a group of tribesmen first encountering members of another tribe heretofore unknown, may be uncertain as to how the new group's existence should be understood within the context of their shared weltanschauung. Members of the new tribe are not yet considered to be moral or amoral. Until an attribution is made, they remain part of the nonmoral realm.[1]

Components of the moral realm are distinguishable from those in the amoral realm by measuring the reaction of a group member to any known artifact, behavior, or statement of belief. While Durkheim relied primarily on the observation of sanctions to reveal the sacred, the approach taken here is broader. Reactions to those components which are part of the moral realm will elicit either a positive or negative moral valuation. They may be received with a certain reverence or sense of awe, or elicit an aversive reaction which incites fear or revulsion. Amoral aspects may elicit emotive responses, such as laughter, pleasure, or even grief, but a morally evaluative aspect will be absent. Some variation in individual responses can be expected, but aggregated responses will reveal fundamental aspects of a group's moral system.

Durkheim observed that the proportion of life interpreted as *sacred* shrinks drastically as a society undergoes industrialization. Aspects of existence perceived as profane realize a corresponding increase during this process. This means that people in modern societies encounter more life experiences and artifacts devoid of religious meaning and perceive them as simply existing. Durkheim referred to this as the process of *secularization*. A similar trend can be described with the new terms defined above. While most every aspect of life is interpreted within the *moral realm* in traditional societies, people in modern societies perceive more parts of life as *amoral*. The result is a good deal less time spent deliberating about the moral meaning of issues and items in modern society. Human beings have much more individual freedom to choose to act according to their own desires, free from criticism, judgment, and negative sanctioning from others. This process might be termed *amoralization* for our purposes, though its close correspondence to the meaning of secularization should be clear. Amoralization may be a more useful term to tease out nuances in moral debates in modern societies as conflicts often involve two or more secular entities; neither of which may invoke a sense of sacred.

Though the proportion of life experiences interpreted within the moral realm generally decreases in modern societies, bitter disputes over what aspects of life *should* be ensconced within the moral realm continue, and may even increase.

---

[1] The concept of the nonmoral here is an application of Collins' (1992) concept of nonrationality.

Foucault (1990), for example, noted an explosion of discourse over sexuality in Victorian England at the same time that sexual behavior presumably decreased. Becker (1963) used the phrase *moral crusade* to characterize organized attempts to convince the general public that certain (amoral) aspects of life should be bedeviled, or interpreted as wrong or bad. Whether sincere or orchestrated, moral crusades in modern societies make heavy use of political and rhetorical devices in order to engender a moral consensus. Moral conflicts in modern society are not only a function of traditional versus modern values, but also have to do with increased competition over a decreasing moralized space and the professionalization of moral suasion. As we will see, successful solutions to moral conflicts are often realized in the increased abstraction of moral principles or ideals.

Having defined key concepts, we now turn to a description of the moral system.

The Bummer of Being Human

Theorists such as Arnold Gehlen, Fredrich Nietchze, Sigmund Freud, Helmuth Plessner and others have challenged the *anthropocentric bias* in evolutionary theorizing. While most theorists begin with an attempt to explain humankind's 'obvious' natural superiority over other species, Gehlen's (1940) philosophical anthropology begins with the supposition that homo sapiens are a defective life form. Gehlen noted what he saw as intrinsic human deficiencies in comparison to other animals: organic primitivism (e.g. poorly developed jaw), lack of a coat or pelt to protect against the elements, the complete helplessness of a newborn, the painfully long period of dependency and maturation, and late sexual maturity. Combined with almost no natural instincts and what might be summarized as an inability to focus, Gehlen offers a theory of society-as-compensation for the inadequacies of human beings. Banding together for survival and developing institutions to direct actions, society offers humans the possibility of collective survival. Shared knowledge and cooperative economic activities help the species to transcend its innate vulnerabilities (in Honneth and Joas 1988).

Biologists like Alexander (1987) also suggest that society makes possible an aggregation helpful in obtaining common resources. Social cooperation facilitates information sharing, predator avoidance and defense, nepotistic investments in kin, and the hunting and killing of otherwise unattainable large prey. Turner (2006) draws on Gehlen's observations of human vulnerability to build his own theory of human rights. Because social institutions tend towards decay, Turner argues, human rights are needed as an ultimate mechanism of protection against vulnerability. While a discussion of human rights at this point is premature, suffice it to say that we too begin here with the observation of humankind's natural vulnerability, but expand beyond it.

Humans have reasons for creating society apart from their natural inferiority. Sociality and interdependency is now a part of our nature, a point demonstrated in Chap. 4. Humans seek the company of others because without it we are left wanting. Loneliness can produce a host of psychological maladies. In addition to protection and connection, society offers *socialization*; a powerful force that unleashes personal potentials that are otherwise locked within a solitary individual. Studies of feral children raised in relative isolation or by wild animals procure evidence of just how emancipating is the process of socialization. Larger societies can create new dangers for human beings in the way of domination, exploitation, and mass death, but they also provide incredible opportunities for personal expression and self-growth simply unavailable in smaller societies. For thousands of years, people have been drawn to urban areas for economic and educational opportunities, art and music. In addition to the need for survival and sociality, then, society has the potential to meet the human needs of self-growth and personal expression. In many ways, the last 12,000 years of human society-building has been a history of deciding whose needs will be met first, most, and at what cost to others.

Nussbaum (2011) develops her capabilities approach by accepting a theory of society that acknowledges the human need for growth and development. Since the best of human achievement and enlightenment has been wrought collectively, Nussbaum suggests that each society needs to address the straightforward question: *what is each person actually able to do and be?* The success of a society, Nussbaum argues, *should* ultimately be measured by the extent to which each individual participant has been provided with opportunities for growth. Sen (2009) provides a similar approach, offering that personal and societal development is about more than opportunities: it is about justice. Though these authors move the dialogue from a descriptive analysis of what a society *is* to what it *should* be, their models presuppose a theory of society based on democratic human need fulfillment. Malinowski's (1948/1992) grounded observations of the Trobriand islanders elicited a similar conclusion.

By focusing on the *ought* question, Nussbaum and Sen also highlight a fundamental challenge faced by societies: how can individuals be motivated to connect with their social self and engage in prosocial behavior upon which society, and one's survival and growth, is ultimately dependent? In addition to the innate human needs for survival, sociality, and growth is a powerful tendency towards selfishness. Dawkins (1976/2006) subordinated all other human tendencies to the survival instinct in his successful book, *The Selfish Gene*. Enthusiastically received by biologists long criticized by the religious right, as well as those eager to find scientific justification for an economic system that produces inequality, Dawkins provided substantial evidence that the human tendency toward 'selfishness' is innate. Thirty years later, Dawkins ruminated as to whether he should have instead chosen the title *The Immortal Gene*, given that the word *selfish* is so laden with moral innuendo. His tome, nonetheless, resonated intuitively with a wide readership. We know our selfishness personally. Social living requires unselfish behaviors like turn-taking, sharing, and give-and-take. The human moral dilemma is thus choosing between our autonomous, but lonely, vulnerable, and incomplete self on the one hand, and our social, secure, connected, growing but interdependent self on the other. Because the autonomous, selfish self is a danger to the integrity of society, human communities create rules and regularized patterns of interacting that prioritize the prosocial choices over that of selfish choices. The social apparatus developed to motivate prosocial behavior is called the *moral system*.

Societal members create a moral system to motivate members to engage in prosocial behavior insomuch as it pertains to ingroup members. Seldom is this done intentionally, at least in traditional societies. Over time, stories emerge that explain the origins of the group; stories that infer a sense of collective purpose and destiny. They impart to individuals an identity and affirm the moral superiority of the group. They articulate for individuals a sense of purpose in relation to the group. These stories help to contextualize the rules of the moral code. Specifically, then, the moral system consists of the following components:

1. **A creation myth**, which explains both the origins of the physical universe inhabited by the social group and the social group itself.
2. **A metaphysic**, or explanation of the meaning of life and one's place in the universe.
3. **A moral code**, or list of behavioral expectations.

Taken together, the components of a moral system are self-reinforcing. They motivate members to engage in prosocial behavior by offering explanations as to why otherwise selfish individuals might engage in altruistic activities. Creation myths invoke a cosmological connection to the universe and infer a special status to the group. They confer a sense of inherent morality and destiny. The moral system provides a connection with other group members that is transcendent of time and space. It ultimately serves to promote social cohesion and the integration of societal members, all of which are needed for the long-term survival of the group.

All religions are examples of a moral system, but only some moral systems take the form of a religion. Though it is often claimed that all societies have some form of religion, the truth of the assertion depends very much on one's definition of religion. Many anthropologists reject the notion that animism is a legitimate form of religion. If true, explaining the existence of morality for the 190,000 years of human history in which animism was the dominant belief system becomes problematic. A focus on moral systems solves this problem, for moral systems are a true cultural universal in that they exist in every society.

The ethnomethodological observation that these constructions logically implode upon close scrutiny reveals the social nature of moral systems. They are meant to provide enough context to motivate individuals to transcend their selfishness and commit themselves to the social group. Searching for deeper meaning or philosophical truths in moral systems eventually leaves many an investigator wanting, with more unanswered questions than when they began. Though selfish, human beings desire connectedness. Cosmologies, metaphysics and moral codes need only be sufficiently cogent to provide an excuse for engaging in cooperative behavior. The true test of their integrity is not in logical acuity or even the empirical validity of presuppositions, but their long-term ability to integrate members into a cohesive whole.

Moral systems are closed. They apply only to members of the same tribe or group that share the same moral system. Members are provided an explanation of the group's origins and their role within it. Because other groups exist outside of the moral system in the nonmoral realm, the moral rules and behavioral prescriptions of the tribe do not apply. This can help explain the historically arbitrary nature of inter-group contact, which has ranged from genocide and enslavement to assimilation and full-fledged acceptance. Because moral systems often incorporate cosmologies and metaphysical claims rooted in immutable truth claims and axioms, they tend towards stasis. Change is often seen as a threat and is perceived to be immoral. Moral systems thus tend to encourage social conservatism. Because a group's survival depends on successful adaptation, members are generally loath to change practices and beliefs that have heretofore served them well. This is why the moniker *traditional society* is so well-earned. While reasonable, conservatism can inhibit the evolution of moral systems more adept at integrating diverse populations into a cohesive whole.

A Theory of Moral Change

Having described a moral system and related concepts, it is now possible to out-line a theory of moral change. Social theorists have identified many catalysts of sociocultural evolution, including climatic changes, technological innovations, economic surpluses, ideological development, and more. Because a change in a moral system is largely adaptive, it almost always follows, rather than precedes, changes in other areas of society. This approach is congruent with Lenski's (2005) ecological-evolutionary approach, but seeks to further explicate the nature of moral change per se. This approach is also in-line with a *cultural materialist* orientation as developed by Harris (1979/2001). Sometimes described as "probabilistic infra-structural determinism" (a misnomer, since probabilistic accounts are not, by defi-nition, deterministic), cultural materialism posits that in almost all circumstances it is the material infrastructure (e.g. environment, technology, demography) that forces adaptive cultural evolution. While most cultural materialists focus on cul-tural change as a whole, the focus here is specifically on moral paradigmatic shifts.

Though infrastructural elements like the environment certainly play a part in the formation of creation stories, we focus on an exposure to *human diversity* as a key instigator of moral change. Human diversity includes a variety of personalities, physi-cal characteristics, cultural practices, dress, and rituals. It includes an array of diverse and conflicting belief systems, world views, and vocabularies used to describe such. Exposure to human diversity poses a fundamental challenge to moral systems by bringing nonmoral aspects of life into the realm of immediate experience. People are confronted with others who are different than they are, who exist outside their moral system, and believe and live in a manner different than they do. Prolonged expo-sure to human diversity can stimulate a collective process whereby individuals must come together, acknowledge the diversity, and render an account of it. The longer a group is exposed to human diversity, the greater the likelihood that the exposure will precipitate a moral crisis. Prolonged exposure to human diversity ultimately taxes the credulity of a moral system. It forces a group to account for the existence of the diversity. As diverse individuals and groups become a part of society, moral codes must be developed to prescribe appropriate reactions to the diversity. If the moral prescriptions include the subordination or mistreatment of diverse groups, rebellion and protest against the moral system by the disenfranchised may be realized.

Successful moral adaptation occurs when moral systems are revised and replaced so as to account for the new reality and integrate new peoples in ways that helps reduce conflict, confusion, and resentment. Thus, the types of moral changes that are most successful over time are those that revise moral stories and principles with increasing abstraction, articulating sophisticated moral precepts that are more inclusive and universal and capable of integrating all members into a cohesive whole. Change in moral systems can at times occur relatively quickly, through social revolution. Conquerors often superimpose their moral system on the vanquished but, unless the diversity is extinguished through physical or cultural genocide, segregation, or assimilation, resentment and friction will be ongoing. Moral change is thus an adaptive mechanism used by social groups to enhance social cohesion and aid in the social integration of its members. Ultimately, more human needs are met in moral systems that better integrate the diversity within.

The primary manner in which societal members experience diversity is through population growth. Growth can be realized either internally or externally, but both facilitate exposure to human diversity. *Internal population growth* is realized when birth rates exceed death rates resulting in a net gain. Internal population growth is frequently the result of technological innovations which increase health and longevity. Internal population growth elicits greater diversity through a wider array of personalities, experiences, and behaviors. In large societies, social strata emerge in which the rights and privileges of some are denied to others. Subcultures and counter-cultures can emerge, which test the limits of moral tolerance and understanding.

External population growth occurs as a group comes into contact with populations different than their own. Historically, external population growth has occurred as a result of trade, conquest, and immigration. New populations are subsumed or amalgamated into political systems of increasing size, such as city-states, nations, and nation-states. Though increasing inequality and social stratification are often the result of population growth, questions of fairness and equality fare prominently in public discourse. Mechanisms of redistribution are often implemented, even in societies with great amounts of inequality. Real or symbolic, these mechanisms indicate an ongoing concern with inequality.

Having described the major components of a theory of moral systems, we are left with the following propositions:

Proposition 1 *Homo sapiens band together to increase their chances of survival and to meet human needs.*

Proposition 2 *A moral system; consisting of a creation myth, a metaphysic, and a moral code, serves to integrate societal members by creating cohesion among group members and motivating pro-social behavior.*

Proposition 3 *Because moral principles originate among groups separately, they may differ from group to group. At the point of initial intergroup contact, the moral principles may not be recognizable across groups, thus intergroup contact can, and frequently does, result in warfare, conflict, enslavement, and subjugation.*

Proposition 4 *Internal and external population growth places environmental stress on the credulity of moral systems as exposure to human diversity makes it increasingly difficult for the existing moral system to successfully integrate all members into society. Members of diverse subgroups may openly challenge their implied inferior moral status, resulting in a decline of social regulation and an increase in social conflict and discord.*

Proposition 5 *Prolonged and intense exposure to human diversity often provokes a moral crisis where support for and belief in the current moral system wanes and alternatives are either suggested or incorporated into daily life.*

Proposition 6 *Over time, successfully adaptive societies increase the chances of the long-term survival of its members by adapting more abstract and universal moral principles which better integrate diverse elements into a cohesive whole, thus achieving a better fit with the realities of their changing social environment.*

References

Alexander, R. D. (1987). *The biology of moral systems.* New York: Aldine de Gruyter.

Becker, H. (1963). *Outsiders: Studies in the sociology of deviance* (pp. 147–153). New York: The Free Press.

Collins, R. (1992). *Sociological insight: An introduction to non-obvious sociology.* New York: Oxford.

Cragun, R. T. (2013). *What you don't know about religion (but should).* Durham, NC: Pitchstone.

Cragun, R., & Kosmin, B. (2013). Repackaging humanism as 'spirituality': Religion's new wedge strategy for higher education. *Free Inquiry, 30*–33.

Cragun, R., Kosmin, B., Keysar, A., Hammer, J., & Nielsen, M. (2012). On the receiving end: Discrimination toward the non-religious in the United States. *Journal of Contemporary Religion, 27*(1), 105–127.

Dawkins, R. (1976/2006). *The selfish gene, 30th anniversary ed.* New York: Oxford University Press.

Didyoung, J., Charles, E., & Rowland, N. J. (2013). Non-theists are no less moral than theists: Some preliminary results. *Secularism and Nonreligion, 2,* 1–20. doi: http://dx.doi.org/10.5334/snr.ai. Accessed 10 December 2013.

Durkheim, E. (1912/1962). *The elementary forms of the religious life: A study in religious sociology* (J. Swain, Trans.). London: Allen & Unwin.

Durkheim, E., & Mauss, M. (1963). *Primitive classification* (R. Needham, Trans.). Chicago: University of Chicago Press.

Foucault, M. (1990). *The history of sexuality* (Vol. 1). New York: Vintage.

Friesen, B. (2013). *Secularizing Durkheim: Implications for human rights.* Paper presented at the American sociological association meetings, human rights roundtable session, August 12, 2013.

Gehlen, A. (1940). Der Mensch. Seine Natur und seine Stellung in der Welt. ERSTAUSGABE. Berlin: Junker und Dünnhaupt Verlag.

Habermas, J. (2008). Notes on a post-secular society. *New Perspectives Quarterly,* 25(4). http://www.digitalnpq.org/archive/2008_fall/04_habermas.html. Accessed 13 December 2013.

Harris, M. (1979/2001). *Cultural materialism: The struggle for a science of culture.* Walnut Creek, CA: AltaMira Press.

Honneth, A., & Joas, H. (1988). *Social action and human nature.* New York: Cambridge University Press.

Hume, D. (1739/1985). *A treatise of human nature.* London: Penguin Classics.

Lenski, G. (2005). *Ecological-evolutionary theory.* Boulder, CO: Paradigm.

Malinowski, B. (1948/1992). *Magic, science, and religion and other essays.* Long Grove, IL: Waveland Press.

Nussbaum, M. (2011). *Creating capabilities.* Cambridge, MA: Belknap.

PEW. (2012a). *Nones on the rise.* PEW Research Religion and Life Project, October 9.

PEW. (2012b, December 18). *The global religious landscape.* PEW Research Religion and Life Project. http://www.pewforum.org/2012/10/09/nones-on-the-rise/. Accessed 13 December 2013.

Sen, A. (2009). *The idea of justice.* Belknap: Harvard, MA.

Turner, B. S. (2006). *Vulnerabilities and human rights.* University Park, PA: University of Pennsylvania Press.

Chapter 3
Moral Systems in Traditional Societies

Useful concepts have the ability to clearly and easily distinguish between what is included in the concept and what is not. If a concept fails in this goal; if most anything can be considered a part of the concept, it loses any analytic utility and is best disposed of. This issue of definitional clarity and conceptual integrity is crucial when examining the nature of religion. Merriam-Webster (2013) offers three possible definitions:

1. the belief in a god or group of gods;
2. an organized system of beliefs, ceremonies, and rules used to worship a god or group of gods;
3. An interest, belief, or activity that is very important to a person or a group.

We can omit the third entry since it refers to religion-as-metaphor, as in the statement: *football is a religion in the USA*. The first two parts of the definition are clearly relevant, and indeed, the first is subsumed in the second. The definition of religion used herein, then, is *an organized system of beliefs, ceremonies, and rules used to worship a god or group of gods*. God-oriented activity becomes the litmus test for distinguishing religion from non-religion. A similar definition would likely be produced by most anyone on the street, so the definition is bolstered by popular usage.

I raise this issue as there is a need to contrast conventional definitions of religion with those used by some academics such as the late Robert Bellah. Drawing from Geertz (1966), Bellah (2011: xiv) defines religion as: "…a system of symbols that, when enacted by human beings, establishes powerful, pervasive, and long-lasting moods and motivations that make sense in terms of an idea of a general order of existence." Bellah continues by remarking that, for him, a belief in gods is *not* the defining aspect of religion. Such a definition vastly broadens the subject matter under investigation (useful for an academic) but risks subsuming more activity and belief under the label of religion than might otherwise be identified. It risks glossing over important nuances in practice and belief. Definitions so broad also risk begging the question, since religious belief and activity is found to be ubiquitous

© The Author(s) 2015
B.K. Friesen, *Moral Systems and the Evolution of Human Rights*,
SpringerBriefs in Sociology, DOI 10.1007/978-94-017-9551-7_3

when defined in this manner. A more focused definition reveals the relationship between religion and society to be far less organic than Bellah's definition would imply. This is especially true when examining hunting and gathering societies.

Hunter-Gatherer Society: Pre-religious Morality

In attempting to describe the difference between "gods" and "sprits" in his tome *The Evolution of God*, Wright (2010: 19) suggests: "This leads us to one of the more ironic properties of religion in hunter-gatherer religion: it doesn't exist." Wright goes on to explain that the understanding of the supernatural in the lives of hunter-gatherers was so qualitatively different than that of modern society it couldn't be considered a religion in any real sense of the term, and certainly not so according to our definition above. The beliefs of hunter-gatherers were unique to each tribe. Christianity is a religion in that common beliefs and practices are found wherever it is practiced. The diverse practices and beliefs of all hunter-gatherers can be categorized only conceptually.

The vast majority of hunter-gatherers embraced a type of belief-system known as *animism*, where wind, trees, animals, rivers, and other familiar items were assumed to have souls and, often, a personality. This practice of attributing the existence of a human-like soul to nonhuman entities, by the way, is quintessentially human. Human beings interact with their environment in ways that involve affect. Because we form emotional attachments to inanimate objects and other species, it is understandable how the attribution of other human-like qualities is achieved. For example, my wife Cheryl has told me of a heated debate she and a classmate had with her priest-professor at the Catholic university she attended as an undergraduate, over the issue of whether or not dogs and cats had souls. Opinions were strong on both sides and no attitudes were changed. I'll admit to having had more than one passionate affair with a car or motorcycle I've owned, and felt guilt out of a sense of betrayal when I sold them.

Related to this projection of human-like qualities on nonhuman objects is the tendency to see human faces in inanimate objects, or *pareidolia*. The evolutionary advantage to pareidolia is the ability to quickly distinguish friendly-faces from non-friendly; a decided asset in a forest or jungle fraught with danger. At times, though, this ability causes us to see faces where none exist. Some have suggested that it is this sensation that stimulates the idea that something else is "out there." The sensation manifests itself in a belief in the existence of spirits in hunting and gathering societies, which in turn evolves into polytheistic belief systems in more complex societies.

For hunter-gatherers, spirits were as familiar as pets, family members, or friends. Some spirits were thought to be mischievous or playful, but their cavorting was rarely perceived as malicious and the consequences of their actions were seldom seen as severe. A belief in spirits helped to offer accounts of why certain things happened and brought a sense of familiarity to the world. Wright notes that most hunter-gatherers did not worship spirits but treated them as one would other acquaintances. One's relationship to "supernatural" entities, therefore, had little to do with moral consequences. Ethical laws stood on their own ground in hunting and gathering societies, reinforced by the traditions and popular opinion of the tribe. "If religion is about morality today," Wright observes, "it doesn't seem to have started out that way" (p. 24).

Social structure existed independently of the animistic beliefs of hunter-gatherers. Still, the three components of the moral system were obvious. Spirits, or a long-gone creator-god played a part in some *creation stories*, but the *moral code* was based upon maintaining good rapport in interpersonal relationships with members of the tribe and with the environment that sustained the life of the group. One's meaningful contribution to the activities of the tribe was the assumed *metaphysic*. Because everything in the tribe's known world was relational, all of life was engulfed in the moral realm. Ancient Hebrew, Wright notes, had no word for "religion." Because societal membership was primarily ascriptive through birth, less energy was needed to maintain the legitimacy or logical consistency of the moral code. As such, the moral system was largely closed; applicable only to group members. Others might be grafted in through marriage or enslavement, but trading with outsiders meant the development of new standards of behavior. Because others groups existed outside of the moral universe in the nonmoral realm, enslavement, subjugation, and murder were possible outcomes of interaction, especially if others were perceived as a threat.

An examination of morality in hunter-gatherer groups thus allows us to make two observations. First, that morality can and does exist apart from religion, and second, that religion and morality were decoupled in most situations for all but the last 12,000 of the 200,000 years of modern homo sapien history. As a species, religion appeared late on the stage, inextricably linked to the development of more technologically complex societies and their incumbent social inequality. The reasons for this are made explicit in the sections that follow.

Horticultural Societies: Religion as Moral System

By 10,000 BCE, some human groups were undergoing a fundamental shift in the way they survived. Environmental pressures likely forced tribes in the Fertile Crescent to rethink their manner of survival, eventually adapting to changing conditions through the practice of farming. Simple horticultural techniques and animal husbandry were eventually incorporated. As noted in Chap. 1, technological innovations such as the domestication of plants and animals and the invention of digging sticks made such a life possible. Diamond (2005) attributes the first emergence of this new form of economic cooperation in the Middle East as a kind of geographic *luck* since the area was rich in resources and domesticable animals. Similar transitions, however, emerged independently soon after in China and Southeast Asia, and later still in Meso and North America.

Internal population growth was experienced as a result of technological changes, sustaining populations in excess of a hundred or more. The division of labor became more complex in these societies as subgroups began specializing in specific tasks. Because of increased food availability and dependability, human communities began accruing food *surpluses* for the first time in a meaningful way. Granaries were developed as a way to store these surpluses for longer periods of time. Surpluses could be used to redistribute to families whose crops or animals did not fare as well as others, but it could be also used to trade with other tribes and societies in exchange for rare and desirable commodities like pottery, new types of food, or spices and clothing. Consensual decision-making in these situations became cumbersome so chiefs and other representatives began to emerge, negotiating on behalf of the tribe in trade and commerce activities. Trading partners often bestowed gifts on the negotiators as a way of inducing rapport and respect; gifts which the negotiators often kept for their own. In time, chiefs and wealthier individuals came to accrue social status and sought to assert their dominance in other aspects of tribal life.

A more specialized division of labor, wealth disparities, and the accrual of political power introduced real social inequality into societies. Some members questioned or resented growing amounts of political and economic inequality, as human beings possess an innate sense of fairness; the subject of Chap. 4. New ideologies had to be developed to legitimize inequality and make palpable to the disenfranchised the new order of things. This required a fundamental revolution in the moral system. Bellah (2011: 178) suggests: "For an upstart to become a legitimate ruler there has to be a reformulation of the understanding of moral community and new ritual forms to express it, so that despotism becomes legitimate authority and therefore bearable by the resentful many who must submit to it." For Bellah, despotism becomes *hierarchy* when legitimacy is achieved.

To be effective, new moral systems had to move the origins of morality away from an intuitive sense of sociability, egalitarianism, and reciprocity, to sources *outside* the individual. Available sources in the cultural repertoire included spirits and, most often, ancestors. Because these entities were seen as supernatural, their gaze was inescapable. Being told that one is being watched by one's ancestors or by a spirit that demands acquiescence to new moral codes becomes an effective way of increasing conformity still demonstrable today (Spiegel 2010). Though the authoritative source of morality is externalized in organized religion, it is not without intrinsic rewards. Some claim that the presence of strong intrinsic reward systems is evidence of an evolutionary predisposition to a belief in God or religion. In a review of the neuroscience literature on the subject, Hammond (2003: 360) suggests that "...religious experiences do not have their own specific subsystem of arousal rewards, but instead piggyback upon processes established before the origin of our species and expanded in our evolutionary formation."

Durkheim (1912/1962) recognized the connection to deep emotions in *Forms* when he described the notion of *collective effervescence* as a collective sense of connection and exhilaration, induced through social ritual. Social experiences like religious activities or the reaffirmation of strong social bonds have been correlated with increases in hormones such as vasopressin (Maclean et al. 1994) and heightened activity in areas of the hypothalamus or amygdala of the temporal lobe. Participants in non-religious social activities, though, have testified to experiencing similar positive emotional states, such as those involved in the rapidly-growing megachurch movement centered around atheist beliefs (Englehart 2013). Still others experience it during patriotic or sports activities; identified by Bellah (somewhat ironically) as *civil religion* (Bellah 2011).

Marshall (2010) offers a theory of sacralization to explain the emergence of religious belief. He suggests that individuals sacralize (i.e. attribute the status of taboo) objects or activities frowned upon by society with which they are tempted to engage. Once the notion of the sacred is created and externalized to the individual, other items invoking temptation are also sacralized. The sacred is thus produced as a means to reconcile the tension between temptation and tradition. Extending this process further, one could see how moral sentiments could be codified into religious sentiments and, eventually, developed into dogma as societies become increasingly complex. Some societies adopt polytheistic belief systems over time, as the power attributed to certain animistic spirits ever increases. Some of these more powerful spirits are said to be concerned with the moral behavior of individuals. To help citizens discern right from wrong, political leaders either declare themselves as having special dispensation from certain deities to discern moral from immoral behavior, or install full-time religious personnel to develop moral dogma in consultation with the political leader. Over time, personal sacrifice and a sense of duty are emphasized as noble and desirable moral attributes— at least for the disenfranchised. Similar processes are used by Marshall (2008) to explain the emergence of a belief in a god and the advent of moral reasoning.

Thus, religious belief and practice becomes more specialized, formalized, impersonal, and demanding as populations increase. Spirits previously thought to live alongside human beings are now thought to be concerned with issues of morality. *Creation stories* evolve that imply the favored moral status of the group among the gods. Idols emerge as both an object of worship and a reminder of the deference, sacrifice, and duty demanded by their *moral codes*. The ultimate source of morality moves from an intuitive sense of right and wrong to moral codes created by political or formal religious leaders claiming special dispensation. Indeed, political and religious leaders increasingly demand preferential treatment and deference, if not outright worship. For simple horticultural and pastoral societies and the agrarian societies that follow, the moral system becomes fully enmeshed with religious dogma and practice. These beliefs almost entirely legitimize the status quo as formal religion is organized into a conservative and homogenizing force.

Still, while demanding much from those on the bottom of society, the social psychological rewards for religious compliance are often said to be rich. Religion offers emotional salve, hope, a sense of righteousness, inclusion, and the motivation to persevere. Equally important, it offers a justification for daily exploitation, without which the reality of such would be unbearable. While this function of religion is not to be underestimated, some view it as a mechanism for reducing the cognitive dissonance experienced by the disenfranchised who witness increasing amounts of inequality. Indeed, Glock et al. (1967) have found empirical support for their Comfort Hypothesis: those less successful in society tend to be *more* religious than those who are more successful. Glock et al. postulate that, denied of societal success and status, the disenfranchised are attracted to the emotional salve and promises of eternal rewards to those who suffer in the here and now.

There are limits to the amount of inequality people will tolerate, however. In his discussion of historical materialism, Marx (1859/1977) identified forms of inequality in archaic societies. Ancient societies were based on a ruling class who enslaved others; while feudalism enabled landowners to exploit serfs for crops, labor, sons (for warfare), and more. According to Marx, each arrangement allowed for the exploitation of one group by those who owned the means of production and each contained the potential for revolution by the exploited. Slave rebellions have taken place in virtually every slave society that has existed (Urbaninczyk 2008). Anthropological observations indicate that resistance to inequality takes many other forms as well. Robbins (2012) illustrates how collective resistance to declining standards of living wrought by globalization has included the use of gossip to deride the reputation of elites, collective resistance, sabotage, worker's strikes, and even outright revolution. Robbins describes how new religious movements can also be seen as reactions to changes in quality of life, illustrated by the materialist-envy cargo cults of New Guinea or the more common utopian/escapist themes expressed movements like the Ghost Dance of U.S. Plains Indians. The latter emerged shortly after Indians were segregated onto reservations. Marx would no doubt see such movements as more symbolic of false consciousness, similar to the plight of those he identified in *The 18th Brumaire of Napoleon Bonaparte* (Marx 1852/1994), but the activities take the form of resistance nonetheless.

Experiences with resistance against inequality illustrate the difficulty of sustaining an egalitarian moral system in the wake of fundamental population growth. Lenski (2005), for example, reviews the existing archaeological evidence to build a case that the ancient Israelites originated as a slave revolt from Egypt. The group fled to land inhabited by Canaanites but initially avoided much conflict by settling in the sparsely populated hills of the area and away from cities. Early Israel was, like most revolutions of the disenfranchised, markedly egalitarian. As their population increased and their presence became more permanent, a growing division of labor and cultural influences from surrounding societies soon saw political power coalesce into the form of a monarchy. The Biblical account suggests it was the people themselves who clamored for a king, even in the face of a reticent God.

Agrarian Societies: Legitimizing Hierarchy

By 3500 BCE, societies in Mesopotamia had grown large enough to be categorized as advanced agrarian. Characterized by a population of thousands and technological accruements like the plow and irrigation, similar societies emerged soon after in Egypt, India, and China. Burgeoning nations undertook activities to conquer and colonize surrounding areas, resulting in large numbers of diverse peoples subsumed under the rubric of the state. Many were brought as slaves to urban centers at the heart of blossoming empires. Others came as merchants and traders. Maintaining rule over conquered areas often required large armies capable of repressing rebellions by brute force. At times even this was insufficient to sustain long-term peace, and was inefficient in terms of time, money, and resources expended. Successful leaders often responded by incorporating increasingly abstract moral principles into their rule which tolerated diversity while demanding acquiescence.

In her sweeping history of the development of human rights, Ishay (2008) notes that several moral codes of antiquity contained within them universal altruistic guidelines applicable to a substantial portion of the human family. Hammurabi's code; the oldest surviving collection of laws dating back to 1771 BCE, sanctioned punishments for those who transgressed the law and discussed how marriages and divorces should be conducted. Likely influenced by other moral codes, the 6th century BCE Cyrus Cylinder of ancient Persia contained elements of religious tolerance and humane principles. This information corroborates with personal reports of visitors from Greece to Persia's Persepolis, describing the city's ethic as tolerant and diverse. Visitors noted social taboos against vomiting or urinating in public, and emphasized truthtelling. Still, Ishay suggests that the formal moral codes of antiquity fell short of true universalism as they were applied only to certain segments of the population. Slaves and women, for example, were often not accorded the same rights and privileges as others. Nor were the same freedoms or process of law granted to people outside of the empire or other political entity.

Though broadening moral and legal codes by political decree created the potential for a more cohesive society on the one hand, it carried the risk of alienating those who firmly believed in the rightness of older, more exclusive moral codes on the other. Conservative moralists gain psychological rewards from a feeling of moral superiority. Change is frequently construed as a loss. Moral conservatism is partly based on an abject primal fear that any change in the system will ultimately threaten the survival of the group as previously-effective traditions are abandoned. Revising moral codes towards inclusivity ultimately draws into question the credulity of the old moral system. The validity of creation myths, the moral superiority of the ruling ethnic group, and even the meaning and purpose of life must now be re-examined.

Rapid moral change implemented at the hands of political leaders could easily produce resentment and fear, which in turn could foment rebellion and backlash. To avert this, political leaders needed legitimacy and moral authority to implement such changes. One solution to this dilemma was the full merger of religious belief with political leadership in the form of an *imperial cult*. By claiming either to be god-incarnate or the one person with the closest connection to god, political decrees would become unquestionable. The system combined theocracy with absolute monarchy. Many advanced agrarian civilizations practiced emperor worship, including ancient Egypt, China, Rome, and Japan. Though effective enough to send more than 250,000 people to their death annually in ritual sacrifices in Mayan society (Harner 1977), imperial cults too had their limits.

The Axial Age

By the first millennium BCE, a number of societies had created conditions ripe for a moral revolution. Societies were now sufficiently large that human beings were arranged into social strata known as castes. Great diversities of people were subsumed in the name of empires, while trade and travel greatly expanded knowledge of the world. The ongoing challenge of rulers was the suppression of revolts by slaves and colonized others. At the same time, an entire class of wealthy and educated elites, freed from the drudgery of the manual labor needed to sustain their own lives, pondered the nature of society, the cosmos, inequality, and one's place in the grand scheme of things. These societies produced combinations of features not found elsewhere, including sophisticated town-planning, advanced metal technology, coinage, and a central government with established mechanisms of international diplomacy. Bellah (2011: 266) suggests that the new socioeconomic realities of complex societies raised new serious questions about the cosmological order: "Where is the king? Where is the god? Why are we hungry? Why are we being killed by attackers and no one is defending us?"

New realities of social inequality also demanded an answer. They produced in many a growing inner dissonance caused by an innate aversion to inequality on the one hand and a growing disparity between entire classes of citizens on the other. Children of the well-to-do needed to be taught beliefs that neutralized the guilt they felt when coming face-to-face with the consequences of grossly unequal social systems of which they were the beneficiary. Imperial cults failed to eliminate challenges for power or rebellions by the disenfranchised. Political leaders pondered how they might get their subjects to act *morally*, as in compliant and happy subjects of the social order.

Philosopher/priests eventually arose to offer suggestions. Scholars since Jaspers (1951) have referred to the period from 800 to 200 BCE as the axial age. Some of the world's most influential thinkers emerged in this period, each pondering the spiritual and philosophical questions related to life, meaning, motivation, and responsibilities to each other. Confucius, Buddha, Lao Tzu, and Zarathustra (in Mesopotamia) lived during this time, along with Socrates and Plato. Aristotle emerged in Greece; a society which found its way to establish a political democracy. Palestine produced the prophets Elijah, Isaiah, and Jeremiah. Each of these thinkers posited different answers regarding the meaning of life, yet many produced ethical statements virtually identical to what is known in the West as the Golden Rule: treat others as you want to be treated. Confucianism, Buddhism, Jainism, Hinduism, Daoism, and Zoroastrianism were founded during this period, while other major world religions found their expression soon thereafter. Each philosopher and religious thinker offered new visions of morality for the complexities of life in highly stratified societies. Some of the movements called for societal reform, opening opportunities to more people or institutionalizing acts of redistribution akin to the Year of Jubilee in Israeli society. More often, the answer focused on finding an inner sense of peace regardless of the circumstances, and in maintaining positive face-to-face relationships. This shifted focus off of the inequitable social order and, too often, inadvertently made new religions a handmaiden of gross inequality and political indifference.

Many powerful political leaders eventually adopted their own versions of these newfound answers to the meaning of life; some through legitimate conversion, others for political expediency. In many cases, the wedding of powerful political states with new religious moral systems with near-universal appeal served to better integrate diverse populations within. After witnessing the human cost of a bitterly destructive war he himself initiated, Ashoka, emperor of the Indian Mauryan Dynasty of the 3rd century BCE, felt remorse and came to embrace Buddhism. His sincere conversion was motivated by his expressed conviction that Buddhism offered the region a basis for political unity. In the Middle East, Judaism had emerged as a characteristically tribal religion. Though it contained stipulations under which gentiles could be "grafted in," its membership criteria was primarily ascriptive. The Christian remodeling of Judaism, in the wake of Peter's revelatory dream, replaced ascription with the *achieved* status of conversion. In time, the Roman Emperor Constantine would convert and make Christianity the official religion of the Roman Empire in 313 CE. Islam would similarly unite disparate populations in the 6th century CE.

The Growth of Monotheism

As growing societies continue to encounter diversity, monotheistic religions become increasingly appealing as a way to unite various peoples under a single god. In *Forms*, Durkheim (1912/1962) argued that a single god becomes the fullest abstract expression of the idealized attributes of society: powerful, righteous, ordered, disciplined, and yet compassionate. To heed god's call was to conform to the status quo and accept one's lot in life. In *Suicide* (1897/1979), Durkheim further elaborated on the critical role society plays in social integration and social regulation. *Social integration* is the extent to which individuals feel connected to others. It is essentially a pleasurable affective state, produced by positive relations with in-group members. *Social regulation* refers to the normative or moral demands placed on an individual by the group. Membership entails the responsibility of following group norms, which results in further positive social relations and the incumbent feelings of positive affect. Noncompliance to the moral rules of society often results ostracism and exclusion; some of the most powerful mechanisms of social control exercised by social groups because of their strong neurosociological implications. Feelings of social isolation; the opposite of integration, result in the development of feelings of *anomie* or social estrangement. Individuals in an anomic state would more frequently feel compelled to commit egoistic suicide as a way to end the constant affective pain produced by feelings of social estrangement and disconnect.

Aside from social ostracism, Durkheim noted the increased likelihood of anomie to be experienced by individuals during times of rapid social change. Changing group morals can confuse individuals, causing them to feel estranged from societal values and, hence, from others. The introduction of attractive yet larger, more abstract norms and mores held the potential for reuniting members of society. At the time of writing, Durkheim believed the new emergent norm in modern societies was the cult of the individual.

For many during the axial age, monotheism provided an answer the sociological question of how to better realize social integration in highly stratified and increasingly diverse societies. The father of the Judeo-Christian-Arab patriarch Abraham was an idol maker who fashioned idols to represent the religious expressions and favored status of individual tribes. After the death of his father, Abraham eventually united those tribes and inherited a rich birthright for claiming a belief in a single god. Years later, Mohammed would personally witness the violent clashes of tribal warfare as each tribe carried its own representative idol. Mohammed eventually smashed the idols in Mecca and united previously warring tribes under the Shahada claim that there is no god but Allah (and Mohammed is the messenger of Allah). A larger, more powerful and single deity provided a new sense of social solidarity and unity between previously disparate peoples.

The roughly 2,600 years that separates these two events illustrates another important aspect of moral revolutions as noted both by Bellah (2011) and Dubos (1968: 270): the past is not dead, but continues to exert influence for extended periods. Nothing is lost, in other words, despite moral paradigmatic shifts. Past beliefs and practices continue to be valued by some, while others are resurrected and gain popularity again later on. A cacophony of calls to morality exists in modern societies, which includes voices from more recent generations as well as the distant past. They are heard, though, both because their voices are superseded by a larger, more abstract moral principle which values freedom of expression and self-determination, and because calls to revert back to a moral system of old ordinarily have limited appeal. Similar to sociocultural evolution, change in moral systems can be slow and uneven. They are rarely linear.

Research on Monotheism

The evolution of moral systems is illustrated in the changing perceptions of the attributes of a creator-god in monotheistic societies. Durkheim (1912/1962) argued that an idealized society is ultimately abstracted in this transcendent, external moral force identified as a deity. Following this logic, deities of larger, more complex societies should be understood to have more powerful and abstract (incomprehensible) attributes than those found in less-complex societies. To remain credible, members of a large, complex society need to envision a more powerful and complex god in order to believe the deity represents a powerful society and has the ability to control all things. Monotheism thus offers a comprehensive system of belief which compels members of society to fully embrace religious values and norms which have the consequence of promoting a sense of social solidarity in the face of growing inequality and diversity.

Research has demonstrated the correlation between the increasing structural complexity of social systems and the perceived attributes of a supreme being. Swanson (1960) analyzed 50 traditional societies found a relationship between the development of monotheism and increasingly complex political organization. Underhill (1975) found both economic and political complexity to have an impact on the development of monotheism, though the former had a greater influence on religious belief. Underhill also observed a corresponding increase in the perceived attributes of a supreme creator and economic complexity. Rowes and Raymond (2003) found a positive relationship between the size of a society and increased beliefs in a god interested in moral behavior. They theorized that an increased emphasis on adherence to moral rules and social cohesion in larger societies is the result of conflict with other societies. Rulers emphasize beliefs related to conformity so as to avoid the costs associated with splitting the society into smaller groups. Moor et al. (2009) documented a correlation between the increasing technological sophistication of more populous societies and references to technological processes in creation stories; aspects that resonate more readily with members of technologically complex societies.

Research reported in Lenski's (1970) work illustrates the basic hypothesis. Population growth increases as economic systems change from hunting and gathering and simple horticultural, to advanced horticultural, and then to agrarian societies. To measure the increased perception of a deity's ability to control all, Lenski conceptualized three categories of increasing power: (1) a god who created the world and left, (2) a god who created the world, continues to hold it together, but is largely uninterested in human affairs, and (3) a god who created the world, holds it together, and is interested moral behavior. The results of the analysis are depicted in Table 3.1. A strong correlation is observed between the type of society

Table 3.1 Type of society by perceived power of supreme creator

Beliefs concerning god or supreme creator (SC)					
Type of society	No concept of SC (%)	Inactive SC (%)	Active, not morally supportive SC (%)	Active, morally supportive SC (%)	Total percent[a]
Hunter gatherer	60	29	8	2	99 % (85)
Simple horticultural	60	35	2	2	99 % (43)
Advanced horticultural	21	51	12	16	100 % (131)
Agrarian	23	6	5	67	101 % (66)
Total					N = 325 societies

[a]Row totals may not add to 100 % due to rounding error [adapted from Lenski (1970: 134)]

(a proxy measure for population size) and the perceived power of a supreme being. As the table illustrates, 60 % of hunting and gathering societies have no concept of a Supreme Creator. Of those that do, the vast majority hold to beliefs of a creator *in absentia*. By contrast, the great majority of agrarian societies (67 %) believe in the most powerful form of a Supreme Creator; one who created, sustains, and is concerned about moral behavior.

Lenski attributed this correlation to changes in technology and communication which in turn impact political organization. Changes in technology also produce increasing diversity through internal and external population growth. Increased diversity creates pressure on a moral system to adapt to the new social reality. Successful societies either adopt a new moral belief system with a greater ability to integrate disparate peoples, or fundamentally alter one or more components of an existing moral system to the same effect. The latter process can be seen in some cases of monotheism. Despite claims of an unchanging, eternal god, historical accounts of the attributes or reported nature of God have clearly varied over time. Modern apologists feel compelled to account for such disparities; particularly if they appear in sacred texts. A cottage industry of apologetic texts has emerged within protestant Christianity, for example, attempting to reconcile observed differences between the God of the Old and New Testaments (e.g. Copan 2011; Lamb 2011).

The information above illustrates how social factors such as population size and technological complexity have influenced changes in the expression of moral systems. While religion did not exist in most hunting and gathering societies, its development coincides with the incumbent population growth and the legitimation of hierarchy in horticultural and agrarian societies. The increasing diversity and social inequality of advanced agrarian societies produced a moral crisis addressed in the axial age; a time when people searched for meaning in the face of counter-intuitive social realities. The research presented here illustrates that this crisis was responded to in many cases by the increased abstraction of moral principles, expressed in the form of religious belief. While successful to a point, the simultaneous growth of the major world's religions brought about untold death and destruction as each moral system demanded a homogeneity of belief at all costs. Given the cost of this stalemate, secular moral systems began to emerge in modernity; a subject taken up in Chap. 5.

References

Bellah, R. (2011). *Religion in human evolution: From the paleolithic to the axial age.* Cambridge, MA: Harvard University Press.

Copan, P. (2011). *Is god a moral monster?* Ada, MI: Baker Books.

Diamond, J. (2005). *Guns, germs, and steel.* New York: WW Norton & Co.

Dubos, R. (1968). *So human an animal.* New York: Scribners.

Durkheim, E. (1897/1979). *Suicide: A study in sociology* (J. Spaulding & G. Simpson, Trans.). New York: The Free Press.

Durkheim, E. (1912/1962). *The elementary forms of the religious life: A study in religious sociology* (J. Swain, Trans.). London: Allen & Unwin.

Englehart, E. (2013, September 22). Atheism starts its megachurch: Is it a religion now? *Salon.* http://www.salon.com/2013/09/22/atheism_starts_its_megachurch_is_it_a_religion_now/. Accessed 24 December 2013.

Geertz, C. (1966). Religion as a cultural system. In M. Banton (Ed.), *Anthropological approaches to the study of religion*, ASA Monographs, 3 (pp. 1–46). London: Tavistock Publications.

Glock, C., Ringer, B., & Babbie, E. (1967). *To comfort and challenge: A dilemma of the contemporary church.* Berkeley: University of California Press.

Hammond, M. (2003). The enhancement imperative: The evolutionary neurophysiology of Durkheimian solidarity. *Sociological Theory, 21*(4), 359–374.

Harner, M. (1977, April). The enigma of Aztec sacrifice. *Natural History, 86*(4), 46–51. http://www.latinamericanstudies.org/aztecs/sacrifice.htm. Accessed 17 December 2013.

Ishay, M. (2008). *The history of human rights.* Berkeley: University of California Press.

Jaspers, K. (1951). *Way to wisdom: An introduction to philosophy.* New Haven, CT: Yale University Press.

Lamb, D. (2011). *God behaving badly.* Downers Grove, IL: IVP Books.

Lenski, G. (1970). *Human societies.* New York: McGraw Hill.

Lenski, G. (2005). *Ecological-evolutionary theory.* Boulder, CO: Paradigm.

MacLean, C., Walton, K., & Wenneberg, S. (1994). Altered responses to cortisol, GH, TSH, and testosterone to acute stress after four months' practice of transcendental meditation. *Annals of the New York Academy of Sciences, 746,* 381–384.

Marshall, D. (2008). *A spandrel called 'god': The case of morality.* Paper presented at the American sociological association meetings, Boston, MA, August.

Marshall, D. (2010). Temptation, tradition, and taboo: A theory of sacrilization. *Sociological Theory, 28*(1), 64–90.

Marx, K. (1852/1994). *The 18th Brumaire of Napoleon Bonaparte.* New York: International Publishers.

Marx, K. (1859/1977). *A contribution to the critique of political economy.* Three Rivers, TX: Progress Publishers.

Merriam-Webster. (2013). Merriam-webster online dictionary. *Religion entry.* http://www.merriam.webster.com/dictionary/religion. Accessed 13 December 2013.

Moor, N., Ultee, W., & Need, A. (2009). Analogical reasoning and the content of creation stories: Quantitative comparisons of preindustrial societies. *Cross-Cultural Research, 43,* 91–122.

Robbins, R. (2012). *Global problems and the culture of capitalism* (5th ed.). Boston, MA: Pearson.

Rowes, F., & Raymond, M. (2003). Belief in moralizing gods. *Evolution and Human Behavior, 24*(2), 126–135.

Spiegel, A. (2010, August 30). Is believing in god evolutionarily advantageous? *NPR.org.* http://www.npr.org/templates/story/story.php?storyId=129528196. Accessed 15 December 2010.

Swanson, G. (1960). *The birth of the gods.* Michigan: University of Michigan Press.

Underhill, R. (1975). Economic and political antecedents of monotheism: A cross-cultural study. *The American Journal of Sociology, 80*(4), 841–861.

Urbaninczyk, T. (2008). *Slave revolts in antiquity.* Berkeley, CA: University of California Press.

Wright, R. (2010). *The evolution of god.* New York: Back Bay Books.

Chapter 4
Biological Underpinnings

New research has greatly added to our understanding of human behavioral propensities which many connect to the study of morality. Evolutionary approaches to human behavior readily acknowledge the existence of innate tendencies in the human species. Evolved psychological tendencies have been well documented in both biological and neuropsychological literatures, including the survival instinct, sex drive, nurturing capabilities towards young children, attraction to aesthetics, and a psychological connection to nature. Innate tendencies towards social bonding and cooperation have also been observed. These proclivities serve as motivational forces and continue to operate even when new learning occurs. Learning is thought to add to instinctual behavior, but cannot replace it. Rare exceptions to these observed tendencies can hardly be taken as evidence of the negation of these observed traits, and can be accounted for either in the evolutionary tendency towards mutation or variability, or other hereditary or environmental influences on the particular organism in question (Pinker 2003). Research suggests that a universal *moral language* may be part of the human condition.

Most sociologists today find the contents of the previous paragraph contentious. Though credible evidence from the natural sciences is incorporated into subfields like the Sociology of Health and Medicine or Biosociology (Hopcroft 2010). Sociology has demonstrated its overall resilience in rejecting or ignoring insights into human behavior from other disciplines. The reasons may be understandable, if not always excusable. Most of the outright rejection of information suggesting innate predispositions is motivated by politics rather than science. Of course, most researchers read studies in their own field, and Sociology is, after all, a field that focuses on society rather than biology. The bigger explanation, though, deals with the incredible dangers of using the authority of a scientific voice to justify racism, sexism, classism, and the like; ideologies of group superiority that have cost the lives of millions in the last 400 years of world history. Modern race-based slavery, the Nazi Holocaust, the subjugation of women, and the widespread sterilization

© The Author(s) 2015
B.K. Friesen, *Moral Systems and the Evolution of Human Rights*,
SpringerBriefs in Sociology, DOI 10.1007/978-94-017-9551-7_4

of the infirm are contemporary examples of draconian movements who justified their activities by the selective and biased use of science. Though thorough critiques of past errors have been produced (Gould 1996; Tavris 1993), racism, sexism, and classism remain dangerous undercurrents in human societies. For some sociologists, validating *any* evidence of innate differences opens a pandora's box of potential dangers. This, despite the fact that authors like Tavris (1993) draw on good quality studies to illustrate ways in which men and women *are* different but argue against the privileging of some traits over others.

If the dangers of overgeneralization or selective interpretation of natural science data are real, so too is the possibility that a sociological approach which ignores quality information from the natural sciences will render itself irrelevant and naïve. The rigor of a negativistic logic in science remains a primary defense against science in the service of ideology, along with interdisciplinary peer review. Negativistic logic begins with the premise that no patterns or causal connections exist until overwhelming evidence to the contrary renders that default position as untenable. Examining information outside of one's field can assist in building more complex models of human behavior that provide a fuller account than those produced in academic silos. The trend towards convergence in science, described in Chap. 1, makes more immediate the challenge for sociologists to read work outside their field and to allow non-sociologists the opportunity to critique sociological work. Researchers outside of one's discipline can be particularly adept at identifying implicit assumptions in behavioral models that need to be made explicit.

I review in this chapter but a small sample of scientific research which appears to demonstrate certain innate human tendencies defined as moral in almost all societies; at least as it pertains to in-group members in good standing with the community. I will avoid committing the naturalistic fallacy by suggesting that what is innate is necessarily good, since certain social situations can also stimulate natural aggressive instincts many would define as bad or dangerous. I simply demonstrate that the themes of equality and cooperation so often finding expression in new social movements are far from random. Such proclivities find their origins deep within the human condition. The process of attributing *value* to innate tendencies of cooperation over aggression in moral systems may indeed be the result of social processes, but they are far from arbitrary. In *Evolution and Human Behavior*, Cartwright (2008: 353) articulates a Darwinian approach in defining morality as "…a set of procedures to help humans, in the face of limited sympathies, personal diversity and competitive instincts, to secure the fruits of cooperation and arrange their equitable distribution." Far more than aggression, cooperation and resource-sharing tendencies among in-group members is what produces a sustainable, cohesive, and rich society.

It is not difficult to see that, across societies, cooperation between in-group members is valued over aggression, and most certainly when it comes to physical aggression. Societies of all sorts have mechanisms in place to limit physical aggression against other in-group members, to allow its expression only in limited circumstances, and to channel it into approved social outlets such as games where the possibility of doing harm to others is limited. The evidence presented here implies certain behavioral tendencies in human beings; evidence that renders as naïve the negativistic assumption that, because moral systems are social constructions, any expression of morality is an equally likely outcome. Theorists must either render an account of the evidence reviewed herein, or resort to a defensive position within the critiques of positivism that imply that science itself is only, and completely, a social construction.

A Theory of Emotions

To label a behavior as moral is to assume a prescriptive stance. This is different than merely observing that certain social stimuli elicit particular emotional states in organisms. Predictive models are complex, but a basic framework of a theory of emotions could go like this. Certain social situations elicit a narrow range of emotional responses in humans. These emotions produce either a positive state (i.e. pleasurable feelings such as joy) or negative state (i.e. uncomfortable feelings such as anger or envy) within individuals. Positive states often produce action as an organism seeks to sustain or reproduce positive emotional states. Negative states motivate actions intended to alleviate the emotional discomfort, and are often accompanied by a sense of urgency. Positive social attention, a feeling of righteousness, power over others, as well as connection and intimacy almost always produce positive emotional states, whereas social disapproval, disconnection, social inequality, and a subordinate status elicit negative emotional states such as guilt, fear, envy, anxiety, or depression.

Interdependency is the hallmark of our emotional makeup, since it is social situations that elicit emotional states in others. Interdependence is further illustrated in the way that even an *absence* of social contact produces negative emotional states like loneliness and depression. Of particular concern are the behaviors that produce a positive emotional state in one member but a simultaneous negative emotional state in another. For example, hoarders may experience a positive emotional state by laying claim to items valued by the group. The same action, however, can elicit feelings of envy among the disenfranchised. Groups are adaptive and will tolerate a certain amount of inequality, but increasing disparity, especially to the point of deprivation, will produce behaviors which challenge the hoarder. These challenges are often collective in nature, taking the form of coalitions.

Strong emotional states are induced most notably in face-to-face situations. Because actions produced by negative emotional states can be socially destructive, human beings and other social species have developed complex abilities to read the emotional state of others. Empathic abilities have evolved where people can read the facial expressions of others and infer their internal disposition. A deep sense of fairness has evolved, making people ever sensitive to differences in material and social status. Because survival depends on the strength of the group, the dominant form of social organization in hunting and gathering societies was egalitarian. Social and material equality reduced the likelihood that negative emotional states and their incumbent destructive social tendencies would manifest themselves in face-to-face societies. Moral systems also evolved which placed value on prosocial activities and devalued anti-social or selfish tendencies. Prosocial activities generated positive emotional states in others and reduced the likelihood of conflict. Moral systems further motivated members of the group to take proactive action to avoid violent confrontations and to offer assistance, solace, consolation, or compensation after a conflict has occurred.

Emotional systems evolved as a way to promote positive behaviors conducive to life in groups. Turner (2000), however, points out that the evolution of emotions also created the potential for horrific acts of violence through the expression of vengeance. Three areas of research are described below to demonstrate the presence of these two-sided dispositions: research on primates and other species, research with human children and babies, and research in experimental economics.

Research on Primates

The present generation is the benefactor of insights gleaned from more than five decades of in-depth research on Great Ape Societies. Great Apes—gorillas, orangutans, chimpanzees, and bonobos—are our closest evolutionary relatives. Because apes are presumably less influenced by the powers of socialization than are humans, it follows that strong behavioral similarities in Great Apes and humans are likely the result of shared genetic and neuropsychological compositions. Longitudinal ethnographic studies of chimpanzees in their natural habitat by Jane Goodall and others (Goodall 1986; Boehm 1999) have observed the routine presence of a host of cooperative practices. Nonhuman primates groom one another, provide support in agonistic encounters, collectively defend access to mates, food resources, and territories from outsiders, and actively donate food to each other. Like humans, most apes live in stable social groups, recognize group members as individuals, and have large brains and good memories. These conditions both increase the need for cooperation and facilitate positive relationships with other community members over time.

Experimental research has likewise confirmed a preference for prosocial behaviors in chimpanzees and other primates. de Waal (2013: 120) describes an experiment in which a chimp could choose between two different colored coins. One coin resulted in a food reward for the chimp alone, while the selection of a second coin resulted in a food reward for both the chimp and another chimp in the same room but separated by a wire screen. Chimpanzees chose the prosocial coin three times for every one time they made the selfish choice. The same experiment with human children produced virtually identical results (de Waal et al. 2008).

In another experiment with capuchin monkeys, Wolkenten et al. (2007) had capuchins exchange a rock for a food reward. A piece of cucumber was accepted by a capuchin if alone in the room, but bedlam would ensue if the capuchin receiving the cucumber observed a second capuchin receiving a more desirable grape in a similar exchange. The capuchin receiving the "lesser" cucumber would often yell and throw the cucumber slice at the experimenter or drop it on the floor, walking away in disgust. Similar inequity aversion has been observed in domestic dogs, where a dog receiving no food reward for a trick would eventually walk away when observing another dog receiving a reward for the same trick (Range et al. 2009).

A wide body of research involving chimps and other non-human primates has produced similar evidence of a preference for fairness and inequality aversion (see, for example, Melis et al. 2009; Brosnan et al. 2011; Bullinger et al. 2011; Proctor et al. 2013). Humans, chimpanzees and capuchin monkeys show similar preferences for the division of rewards, which researchers attribute to a shared evolutionary history. Research also indicates the evolution of neural networks which elicit positive emotional rewards for prosocial behaviors and negative emotional rewards for anti-social behaviors. Chang et al. (2012) found positive neural activity in the orbitofrontal cortex of rhesus monkeys when giving juice to a companion, but not when receiving such. Evidence from neuroscience also demonstrates that the anticipation of negative emotional states such as guilt can lead to cooperative behavior. In this instance, the behavior is guilt-aversive (Chang et al. 2011). Other primate research has shown that chimpanzees punish others who steal food from them (Jensen 2007). Drawing on years of observations of the chimpanzees at Gombe, Boehm (1999) argues that the prevalence of egalitarianism among non-human primates and human hunter-gatherers is that the weapon of the disenfranchised has always been collective rebellion, especially when the hoarding by the haves results in absolute deprivation of the have-nots. With chimpanzees, the most frequent collectivized sanctioning occurs when a dominant male has monopolized sexual access to females.

Despite these observations, caution must be exercised when inferring root causes of human behavior from research on primates. Humans are obviously unique among primates in many ways, and behavior can differ considerably even between different species of Great Apes. Indeed, de Waal (2013)'s research on bonobos earned him considerable notoriety as he documented the species' unique proclivity for indiscriminate sexual relations. Further, what may be instinctual in some species may be learned in others. Though research presented here illustrates that prosocial behavior among non-human primates is widespread, some studies suggest it is more likely to be expressed in certain ways. Silk (2007) notes that cooperative behavior is more likely to be exhibited between kin relations, though cooperation among nonkin is not infrequent. Brosnan's (2011) theory of primate cooperation is that aversion to inequity is an evolutionary mechanism developed to promote successful long-term cooperative relationships among non-kin. Work in the biological sciences continues to investigate the root causes of behavioral similarities between humans and other primates.

Research with Babies and Children

Research with young children continues to affirm an aversion to inequality (Fehr and Rockenbach 2008; Gummerum et al. 2010; Rochat et al. 2009). Though 3 and 4 year olds often act selfishly, older children have been observed discarding a resource to avoid inequality (Shaw and Olson 2012), and weighing the relative worth of resources (Shaw and Olson 2013) and merit (Kanngiesser and Warneken 2012) to facilitate equitable distribution. Five to eight-year olds prefer to develop and follow impartial rules regarding resource allocation (Shaw and Olson 2013). Researchers continue to investigate the conditions under which behaviors demonstrating a desire for fairness and/or inequity aversion are most likely to be expressed. McAuliffe et al. (2013), for example, compared the rejection rates of unequal offers among children ages five through nine. Disadvantageous distributions were rejected at a higher rate when the larger amounts would go to a peer as opposed to simply not being allocated. Advantageous allocations were rejected almost exclusively in the social context, suggesting that social situations are an important stimulus in inequity aversion; particularly where one is advantaged over another person.

More controversial is the growing body of recent research with babies; much of which appears to affirm innate preferences for fairness at early ages (Sloane et al. 2012; Geraci and Surian 2011). Since emotional states are inner non-observables and language skills are undeveloped in infants, researchers rely on the correct interpretation of nonverbal cues to infer preferences. Indicators used are the amount of time a baby spends staring at an object, whether the child reaches for an object, and the facial expressions exhibited when staring at an object. The replicability of findings across studies with infants suggests that *some* underlying concept is indeed being measured.

Research with infants is also controversial because of its implications regarding the human condition. If the data are valid, these studies challenge dominant child development paradigms in both sociology and psychology. Socialization theories focus on the impact of interactions with parents and other agents in internalizing prosocial norms, while approaches in cognitive psychology emphasize the developmental stages at which children are thought to develop abilities to think in abstract moral terms. Both of these processes are thought to take years to develop. New experimental designs elicit results that seem to affirm an innate preference for fairness in very young children (Olson and Spelke 2008) and even infants (Premack 2007).

Research reported in Bloom's (2013) book *Just Babies* adds additional insight. Drawing from years of experiments with babies aged 3 months to 2 years, Bloom concludes that innate moral intuitions can be brought to light under the right circumstances. In a series of experiments, Bloom and his colleagues show babies a puppet show in which one puppet assists a second puppet who needs help, while a third puppet inhibits the second from pursuing their goal to open a box. After the show, the "good" and "bad" puppets are brought before the baby in equidistant proximity. The majority of babies stare longer at the former puppet than the latter. Over 75 % of babies capable of reaching for an object reached for the "good" puppet. Researchers infer that babies are attracted to puppets who exhibit prosocial behavior.

In another set of experiments, babies witness the same scenario, but the puppet now in need of assistance had previously been seen acting in an anti-social manner. This time, more than 80 % of babies reached for the puppet that inhibited the anti-social puppet from opening the box, as opposed reaching for the puppet who offered assistance. Researchers conclude that babies prefer the puppet that punished the anti-social character. In a recent review of the research with infants, Hamlin (2013) concludes that the collective results of such research suggest that human morality is rooted in human nature.

Human infants require a capacity for empathy in order to respond to the experimental stimuli provided in Bloom's study. Physical evidence of the existence of mirror neurons was first established as recently as 2010 (Mukamel et al. 2010), though speculation of the existence of such preceded the discovery by at least a decade. Mirror neurons aid individuals in facial recognition and interpreting what others are feeling on a visceral level. Human beings who witness pain in others often form facial expressions that indicate the experience of pain themselves; thus "mirroring" the pain others are feeling. These facial expressions often form unconsciously on the face of the witness but indicate the presence of empathy. While most human beings are capable of feeling empathy, Bernhardt and Singer (2012) note that empathy is highly contextual. Perceived fairness of a situation can influence empathic emotions, as can group membership. Studies in social psychology have long noted that humans are more likely to feel empathy towards those they perceive to be similar to themselves (DeLamater and Myers 2007, Chap. 11).

Additional research by Bloom (2013) uncovered behavioral trends in babies and young children showing a preference for those they perceived to be similar to themselves, even with something innocuous as preference for the same type of snack. Bloom infers from these findings an inherent bias towards the in-group; an evolutionary adaptive mechanism for fidelity to the group upon which one's survival depends. Implications of the converse, of course, is that there is a natural inclination for dislike, distrust, or even hatred of those we perceive to be different than ourselves. Greene (2013) constructs a theory of human beings as essentially functioning at the emotional level of what he refers to as a *moral tribe*; a group of human beings whose innate preferences are to those within their group. Reason and socialization can train individuals to deny or place limits on these initial emotional responses to social situations, and even transcend them. Nonetheless, they remain part of the emotional composition of humans that we continue to negotiate .throughout our lives.

Although human beings can learn to identify with large groups, as exhibited in patriotic displays to nation-states, there is a possibility of a biological preference for smaller social groupings. Dunbar (1993) infamously estimated the preferred group size for humans to be between 100 and 230 by correlating the size of the neocortex in various social species with the average group size observed for their species. Noting a correlation between neocortex size and group size, Dunbar reasoned that the ability to maintain group cohesion and integrity is limited by the information-processing abilities of the neocortex. Extrapolating to human beings, Dunbar surmised that human beings would feel most comfortable embedding themselves in communities averaging 150 members.

Despite research that appears to demonstrate a preference for fairness in infants, researchers have long observed behaviors interpreted to be selfish among children between the ages of five and seven. Bloom observed the same, but noticed that a concern for relative gain far outweighed gains measured in an absolute sense. Children consistently demonstrated a preference for outcomes where they received more of something than another hypothetical child, even when the alternative choice would provide them with double or triple of the same thing but would result in an equal allocation to the hypothetical child. More than a display of selfishness, such findings demonstrate a preoccupation among 5–7 year olds with social comparison. By 8 years of age, however, the need to have more than others is replaced with a concern for equity. By nine or ten, more children choose outcomes that provide a *greater* amount of resources to the hypothetical child than they choose for themselves. Researchers attribute these choices by older children to the impact of prosocial socialization, though it is possible that 8 or 9 year olds begin to realize that choices perceived as selfish can have painful social consequences. Rejection has been demonstrated to elicit psychological pain as great as physical pain (Winch 2013). Anticipation of such may also motivate children to transcend their desire for social status in favor of more prosocial choices.

Critics are quick to point out that inferences made from the behavioral observations of babies and young children may be misinterpreted. Assuming that prolonged eye contact or reaching for certain puppets ultimately require inferences to inner affective states that are ultimately unobservable. Further cross-cultural studies need to be conducted to see if children in other cultural contexts act in a similar manner. Still, the existing research with infants appears to validate the presence of a preference for prosocial behaviors. Children aged five to seven more frequently choose outcomes where they accumulate more resources than others, but this tendency largely dissipates by age eight or nine as prosocial choices tend to dominate. Altruistic choices are increasingly observed among older children, where children choose to receive less resources than a hypothetical child. The consistency of results suggests some inner disposition could well be the root cause.

Experimental Economics: The Ultimatum Game

Cross-cultural research is another way to potentially distinguish innate tendencies from those inculcated from society. Versions of the ultimatum game have been used for more than a decade to test the salience of a concern for fairness. The experiment is conducted with two recruits. One person, designated as the "Proposer," is given a sum of money or other desirable medium of exchange. The

Proposer has one opportunity to make an offer to the second person to share a proportion of their tangibles. If the second person accepts the offer, the proposed distribution is made. If the offer is rejected, neither individual receives anything.

Classic economic theory would predict that the second person would accept *any* offer greater than zero from the Proposer, since acceptance would mean leaving the game with more than they had before. In reality, offers of less than 20 % are almost universally rejected, whereas acceptance rates continue to increase as offers approach a 50 % split of the assets. Aversion to gross inequity seems to override any concern for net personal gain on the part of the individual who accepts or rejects the offer. Proposers, on the other hand, may be motivated to make more generous offers either out of a genuine distain for too much inequity (fairness) or out of fear that their proposal will be rejected and they will end up with nothing (selfishness). In the Dictator Game; a variant of the Ultimatum Game where all proposals must be accepted unilaterally, proposers still made more generous offers than a selfish model would predict (Camerer and Thaler 1995).

A substantial body of similar research has emerged in recent years (Fehr and Schmidt 1999; Dawes et al. 2007; Loewenstein et al. 1989; Davis and Holt 1993). Sometimes called the Ultimate Bargaining Game, results have been replicated in a variety of cultures and under a variety of conditions (Tompkinson and Bethwaite 1995; Bolton and Zwick 1995; Cameron 1999) with similar results. Henrich et al. (2001) and Ensminger and Henrich (2013) attribute a degree of cross-cultural variation in outcomes to economic organization, but acknowledge the findings differ by degree rather than kind. Other social factors may also influence outcomes, as evinced in playing the ultimatum game with chimpanzees (Proctor et al. 2013).

Nonetheless, recent research has provided evidence of a neuropsychological basis of reward for equitable offers in humans (Tricomi et al. 2010), as well as other species (Proctor et al. 2013). An aversion to inequality may well be an evolved tendency in humans to reinforce cooperation. This tendency facilitates the development of cultural norms based on an overall sense of equality and fairness. Over time, a social group develops a moral system which reinforces basic notions of equality and cooperation in the traditions and stories of the group. This may help explain why egalitarian forms of social organization in face-to-face societies predominated for well over 100,000 years of human evolution (Gurven 2006), and why more egalitarian forms of governance were re-established after the French and American revolutions.

It should be evident from the research presented in this chapter that human beings have behavioral predilections towards sociality, empathy, fairness, and an aversion to inequity. Considering the evidence, the suggestion by Greene (2013) and others that certain social situations elicit strong tribal positive and emotional responses in most humans is not without merit. Humans are a social species. Positive social relationships remain one of the most powerful predictors of personal happiness (Diener and Seligman 2002). The corollary to this is that distrust for out-group members remains strong. While witnessing the painful experiences of other in-group members may elicit feelings of empathy, *schaudenfreude*—feelings of joy induced at the misfortune of others—is particularly acute when the pain is experienced among members of an out-group (Cikara et al. 2011).

Biological explanations for the human preoccupation with fairness and egalitarianism are informative. They help explain these recurring themes in human history, even to the point of fomenting political revolutions. Taken together, the evidence compels social constructionist theories of society to be qualified, as the forms societies have taken are hardly arbitrary. Constructionists have difficulty procuring credible explanations for the independent global transitions to settled agricultural life, the stratification of larger societies, the questioning of the meaning of life and society during the axial age, and the general evolution of religious beliefs over time, moving from polytheistic to monotheistic expressions. An evolutionary perspective helps shed light on these transitions. It can also inform the interpretations of social science studies. Hauser (2006) and his colleagues surveyed over 200,000 diverse individuals from around the globe, asking them to respond to simple moral dilemmas. More than 90 % of respondents produced uniform responses regarding basic issues of right and wrong. Few of them could explain how they had arrived at their conclusions.

Still, biology is not destiny. Humans can, and routinely do, transcend such emotional impulses through techniques like reason, tradition, or a sense of duty. Lenski's (2005) eco-evolutionary theory notes that biological processes and instincts play a lesser role in determining human behavior in modern societies as reason and a capacity for learning plays an increasingly influential role in human affairs and social organization. In developing a theory of morality, I reiterate that the content of this chapter should in no way be construed to suggest that what is natural is necessarily moral. Ape societies; presumably influenced more by biological forces, are hardly idyllic. Aside from egalitarian tendencies, they are also marked by systems of rigid hierarchy, violent revolutions, and brutal repression (Boehm 1999).

Demonstrating the existence of certain emotive or behavioral predilections is informative, but simply describes what *is*. To design a society that, say, seeks to produce the utilitarian vision of sustained positive emotive states across a large number of individuals shifts the focus from what is to what *ought* to be. Bookshelves today are filled with such attempts (e.g. Corning 2011). Assuming that these innate predilections are necessarily *moral*, as Alexander (1987) suggests in his book *The Biology of Moral Systems*, does as much to obfuscate questions about morality as all-inclusive definitions of religion. Morality *is* a social construct, but one that many wish to be informed by what we know intuitively. Indeed, I will argue in the subsequent chapters that rights-based morality in modernity is such an example. Societal structures and processes can be designed to elicit greater or lesser amounts of positive sentiment in its members, just as much as societies can be designed to produce an inordinate amount of wealth in the hands of very few members. The choice to do either illustrates the socially constructive process of choosing to value certain outcomes over others. Some outcomes will produce more positive sentiment, but it is the members of a particular society that ultimately make the choice. Nature reveals no metaphysic.

Finally, the malleable and diverse nature of humankind must be considered. The burgeoning field of *epigenetics*—the study of how experiences of a single individual can alter the expression of genes within their own lifetime—illustrates the dynamic ongoing interplay between environment and organism. At least some aspects of human nature are in a state of flux, and increasingly under pressure to adapt as more frequent technological and environmental changes occur. Despite its ultimate intentions, a moral system that embeds itself upon the assumption of an invariant human nature could well be doomed to failure. Similarly, social structures predicated on the simplistic assumption that all humans are alike are unlikely to succeed. Diversity is a central evolutionary mechanism that ultimately enables a species to better adapt to changing environments. Because nature produces variation, it can further be expected that a greater diversity of people; by way of personality, sexual orientation, or other characteristics, will be present in larger societies. Any adaptive social system will not only need to be dynamic, but will need to create integrative mechanisms for a wide diversity of people. Until now, moral systems (religious and others) have tied morality to essential, immutable, and unchanging truth claims; claims that quickly erode in the fast-paced change of modern societies. This might help explain the decline of interest in religion in recent years, along with the development of secular systems of morality. In modernity, the latter find their fullest expression in the constitutions of modern nation states.

References

Alexander, R. D. (1987). *The biology of moral systems*. New York: Aldine de Gruyter.

Bernhardt, B., & Singer, T. (2012). The neural basis of empathy. *Annual Review of Neuroscience, 35*, 1–23.

Bloom, P. (2013). *Just babies: The origins of good and evil*. New York: Crown Publishers.

Boehm, C. (1999). *Hierarchy in the forest*. Cambridge, MA: Harvard University Press.

Bolton, G., & Zwick, R. (1995). Anonymity versus punishment in ultimatum bargaining. *Games and Economic Behavior, 10*, 95–121.

Brosnan, S. (2011). A hypothesis of the co-evolution of cooperation and responses to inequity. *Frontiers in Neuroscience, 5*, 43.

Brosnan, S., Parrish, A., Beran, M., Flemming, T., Heimbauer, L., Talbot, C., et al. (2011). Responses to the assurance game in monkeys, apes, and humans using equivalent procedures. *Proceedings of the National Academy of Sciences, 108*(8), 3442–3447.

Bullinger, A., Wyman, E., Melis, A., & Tomasello, M. (2011). Coordination of chimpanzees (*Pan troglodytes*) in a stag hunt game. *International Journal of Primatology, 32*(6), 1296–1310.

Camerer, C., & Thaler, R. (1995). Anomalies: Ultimatums, dictators and manners. *Journal of Economic Perspectives, 9*(2), 209–219.

Cameron, L. A. (1999). Raising the stakes in the ultimatum game: Experimental evidence from Indonesia. *Economic Inquiry, 37*(1), 47–59.

Cartwright, J. (2008). *Evolution and human behavior* (2nd ed.). Cambridge, MA: MIT Press.

Chang, S., Gariépy, J-F., & Platt, M. (2012). Neuronal reference frames for social decisions in primate frontal cortex. *Nature Neuroscience. 16*, 243–250. doi:10.1038/nn.3287.

Chang, L., Smith, A., Dufwenberg, M., & Sanfey, A. (2011). Triangulating the neural, psychological, and economic bases of guilt aversion. *Neuron, 70*(3), 560–572.

Cikara, M., Botvinick, M., & Fiske, S. (2011). Us versus them: Social identity shapes neural responses to intergroup competition and harm. *Psychological Science, 22*(3), 306–313.

Corning, P. (2011). *The fair society*. Chicago, IL: University of Chicago Press.

Davis, D., & Holt, C. (Eds.). (1993). *Experimental economics*. Princeton: Princeton University Press.

Dawes, C., Fowler, J., Johnson, T., McElreath, R., & Smirnov, O. (2007). Egalitarian motives in humans. *Nature, 446*, 794–796.

de Waal, Frans. (2008). Putting the Altruism Back into Altruism: The Evolution of Empathy. *Annual Review of Psychology, 59*, 279–300.

de Waal, Frans. (2013). *The bonobo and the atheist*. New York: W. W. Norton & Co.

DeLamater, J., & Myers, D. (2007). *Social psychology* (6th ed.). New York: Wadsworth.

Diener, E., & Seligman, E. (2002). Very happy people. *Psychological Science, 13*(1), 81–84.

Dunbar, R. (1993). Coevolution of neocortical size, group size and language in humans. *Behavioral and Brain Sciences, 16*(4), 681–735.

Ensminger, J., & Henrich, J. (2013). *Experimenting with social norms*. New York: Russell Sage.

Fehr, B., & Rockenbach, B. (2008). Egalitarianism in young children. *Nature, 454*(7208), 1079–1083.

Fehr, E., & Schmidt, K. (1999). A theory of fairness, competition, and cooperation. *Qualitative Journal of Economics, 114*, 817–868.

Geraci, A., & Surian, L. (2011). The developmental roots of fairness: Infants' reactions to equal and unequal distributions of resources. *Developmental Science, 14*(5), 1012–1020.

Goodall, J. (1986). *The chimpanzees of Gombe: Patterns of behavior*. Cambridge, MA: Belknap.

Gould, S. (1996). *The mismeasure of man*. New York: W.W. Norton & Co.

Greene, J. (2013). *Moral tribes: Emotion, reason, and the gap between us and them*. New York: Penguin.

Gummerum, M., Hanoch, Y., Keller, M., Parsons, K., & Hummel, A. (2010). Preschoolers' allocations in the dictator game: The role of moral emotions. *Journal of Economic Psychology, 31*, 25–34.

Gurven, M. (2006). The evolution of contingent cooperation. *Current Anthropology, 47*, 185–192.

Hamlin, K. (2013). Moral judgment and action in preverbal infants and toddlers: Evidence for an innate moral core. *Current Directions in Psychological Science, 22*(3), 186–193.

Hauser, M. (2006). *Moral minds: How nature designed our universal sense of right and wrong*. New York: Ecco.

Henrich, J., Boyd, R., Bowles, S., Camerer, C., Fehr, E., Gintis, H., et al. (2001). In search of homo economicus: Behavioral experiments in 15 small-scale societies. *American Economic Review, 91*(2), 73–78.

Hopcroft, R. (2010). *Sociology: A biosocial introduction*. Boulder, CO: Paradigm.

Jensen, K. (2007). Chimpanzees are vengeful but not spiteful. *Proceedings of the National Academy of Sciences, 104*(32), 13046–13050.

Kanngiesser, P., & Warneken, F. (2012). Young children consider merit when sharing resources with others. *PLoS ONE, 7*(8), e43979. doi:10.1371/journal.pone.0043979.

Lenski, G. (2005). *Ecological-evolutionary theory*. Boulder, CO: Paradigm.

Loewenstein, G. F., Thompson, L., & Baserman, M. (1989). Social utility and decision-making in interpersonal contexts. *Journal of Personality and Social Psychology, 57*, 426–441.

McAuliffe, K., Blake, P., Kim, G., Wrangham, R., & Warneken, F. (2013). Social influences on inequality aversion in children. *PLoS ONE, 8*(12), e80966. doi:10.1371/journal.pone.0080966.

Melis, A. P., Hare, B., & Tomasello, M. (2009). Chimpanzees coordinate in a negotiation game. *Evolution and Human Behavior, 30*(6), 381–392.

Mukamel, R., Ekstrom, A., Kaplan, J., Lacoboni, M., & Fried, I. (2010). Single-neuron responses in humans during execution and observation of actions. *Current Biology, 20*(8), 750–756.

Olson, K., & Spelke, E. (2008). Foundations of cooperation in young children. *Cognition, 108*(1), 222–231.

Pinker, S. (2003). *The blank slate: The modern denial of human nature*. New York: Penguin.

Premack, D. (2007). Foundations of morality in the infant. In O. Vilarroya, I. Form, & F. Argimon (Eds.), *Social brain matters: Stances on the neurobiology of social cognition* (pp. 161–167). New York: Rodopi.

Proctor, D., Williamson, R., de Waal, F., & Brosnan, S. (2013). Chimpanzees play the ultimatum game. *Proceedings of the National Academy of Sciences, 110*(6), 2070–2075.

Range, F., Horn, L., Viranyi, Z., & Huber, L. (2009). The absence of reward induces inequity aversion in dogs. *Proceedings of the National Academy of Sciences, 106*(1), 340–345.

Rochat, P., Winning, A., & Berg, B. (2009). Fairness in distributive justice by 3- and 5-year olds across seven cultures. *Journal of Cross-Cultural Psychology, 40*, 416–442.

Shaw, A., & Olson, K. (2012). Children discard a resource to avoid inequity. *Journal of Experimental Psychology, 141*(2), 382–395.

Shaw, A., & Olson, K. (2013). All inequality is not equal: Children correct inequalities using resource value. *Frontiers in Psychology, 4*, 393.

Silk, J. (2007). The strategic dynamics of cooperation in primate groups. *Advances in the Study of Behavior, 37*, 1–42.

Sloane, S., Baillargeon, R., & Premack, D. (2012). Do infants have a sense of fairness? *Psychological Science, 23*(2), 196–204.

Tavris, C. (1993). *The mismeasure of woman*. New York: Touchstone.

Tompkinson, P., & Bethwaite, J. (1995). The ultimatum game: Raising the stakes. *Journal of Economic Behavior & Organization, 27*(3), 439–451.

Tricomi, E., Rangel, A., Colin, F., Camerer, J. P., & O'Doherty, J. (2010). Neural evidence for inequality-averse social preferences. *Nature, 463*, 1089–1092.

Turner, J. (2000). *On the origin of human emotions: A sociological Inquiry into the evolution of human affect*. Stanford: Stanford University Press.

Winch, G. (2013). *Emotional first aid: Practical strategies for treating failure, rejection, guilt, and other everyday psychological injuries*. New York: Hudson Street Press.

Wolkenten, M., Brosnan, S., & de Waal, F. (2007). Inequity responses of monkeys modified by effort. *Proceedings of the National Academy of Sciences, 104*(47), 18854–18859.

Chapter 5
Secularizing Morality

Respect for tradition and deference to a political authority believed to be established by the supernatural found its fullest expression in advanced agrarian societies. Magnificent places of worship were erected, partly to invoke divine blessing on the ruling elite and part evidence of such. Economic inequality was solidified by way of permanent social castes. For the millions of people on the lowest rungs of a supposedly civil society, life was nasty, brutish, and short. Many were taught that suffering was a virtue which would produce new spiritual insights and rewards.

Yet despite all attempts to create a static social order, changes and challenges continued to procure questions regarding the integrity of a moral system which married polity with religion. At times the professional religious class periodically questioned, or even condemned, the decisions of emperors and kings. Ongoing demand for tithes, for sons for warfare, or payment for indulgences, raised questions as to the legitimacy of these practices. Constant warfare, even between districts who shared the same religion, raised questions regarding the moral nature of the conflict. Equally important, the random and arbitrary exercise of power against the powerless invoked strong passions of resistance and injustice.

In some ways, one might interpret the stumbling into modernity as an assertion of the need for greater equality and protection from the arbitrary whims of rulers. Pressure from English nobles succeeded in limiting the powers of King Henry I in the 1100 CE *Charter of Liberties*. This *Charter* later inspired the adoption of the 1,215 *Magna Carta*, further limiting the discretionary powers of royalty and guaranteeing that freemen could be punished only as they were in direct violation of law. Dozens of acts similar to the *Magna Carta* preceded it in time (Holt 1992). Still, by recognizing the rule of law, it has come to be seen as a formative document used to protect people from the arbitrary actions of their rulers.

If moral systems take the form of religions in traditional societies, the rise of a secular moral system, articulated in the form of a constitution and embedded in national law is the purview of modern societies. The precursors of this secularizing trend include the preindustrial merchant societies of the world. Various regimes,

© The Author(s) 2015

B.K. Friesen, *Moral Systems and the Evolution of Human Rights*,
SpringerBriefs in Sociology, DOI 10.1007/978-94-017-9551-7_5

including the Golden Age of Islam in the 8th–13th centuries, encouraged humanistic, rational, and scientific thought. Religious tolerance and a growing secularism, at least in some parts of society, was the result (Kraemer 1992; Goodman 2003). Lapidus (1992) describes how the realities of governing complex Islamic countries even during Islam's Golden Age or the Ottoman Empire brought forth new political realities that saw the increasing separation between the political responsibilities of the Caliphate and religious communities who were regarded as the true keepers of the faith. The insights and successes wrought by the use of science and rationalism in the service of empire eventually found their way to the West.

Simultaneous social, economic, and technological changes in the 17th and 18th centuries combined in Europe to give gradual primacy to the use of reason and science over authority and tradition as ways of knowing. To be sure, increasing intercultural contact through world exploration and colonization efforts helped fuel this secular moral shift. Empire had always been the truest fulfillment of the moral system of advanced agrarian societies. The notion of a culturally homogeneous world, with unhindered access to all resources and all people incorporated under a single moral system, had been the catnip of ruling elite and moral absolutists alike, who saw empire as the logical fulfillment of ethnocentric beliefs. Even in modernity, these aspirations persisted. The historical experience of empire, though, teaches that a global empire has been, as yet, unattainable, and that large empire is inevitably unsustainable in any case. Great diversity invariably spawns challenges to power, while the abuse done in the name of empire raises questions about its moral legitimacy. During the time of European hegemony in the Americas, discussions abounded regarding the morals and manners of the indigenous peoples, including the Conquistadors' harsh treatment of them (Pagden 1982). It would not be until the decline of the British Empire that an even newer moral system would gain serious credibility in the West.

Social revolutions and conflict provided a sign that the moral systems of agrarian societies was breaking down. Using reason to question the legitimacy of exploitative and unequal practices of the Christian church led to the Protestant Reformation of the 1500s. A constitutional monarchy replaced royalty in the English Glorious Revolution of 1688. The English Bill of Rights was adopted in the following year, ensuring English subjects a modicum of redress to the monarchical abuse of power. It established the makings of a representative democracy and later served as inspiration for the U.S. Bill of Rights. These limitations on what was previously thought to be the divine right of kings increased the relative power of the average subject and created, in some sense, a certain legal equality.

Such changes, accompanied by the increasing application of science and logic to human affairs, had serious implications. Once reason had been freed from the paradigmatic parameters of tradition and immutable religious claims, universal ideas such as egalitarianism and democracy found fuller expression in the Enlightenment. Continuing warfare brought about new theorizing about the relationship of man and society by Hobbes, Machiavelli, Rousseau, and others. Letting go of the belief that the social order was God-ordained eventually gave birth to the discipline of Sociology, which aspired to use the scientific method to aid in the pursuit of designing better societies. Though not perceived as such at the time, the principles embodied in the series of European peace treaties signed in Osnabrück and Münster in 1648 set in place the political structures under which morality would come to be defined in the modern age. Known as the *Peace of Westphalia*, the treaties established modern nation-states as sovereign, allowed the leaders of nation-states to determine the expression of religion within its borders, and introduced a principle of non-intervention in political affairs by external actors. The reaction of the Vatican to the treaties was swift and unequivocal condemnation, but it resonated with the many political actors involved. It decreased warfare between European states, but did nothing to stem the growing violence in the nonmoral realm of the New World. It was there that a new moral order; the notion of rights, would receive fuller expression.

Rights as the New Moral System

The American and French revolutions embodied the principles of the Enlightenment (Ishay 2008). By adopting a rational and secular Constitution, the U.S. excused itself from the monarchical systems of old to focus more overtly on the needs of the people. "We the people…" it began. The French revolution soon followed, with the call to liberté, egalité, et fraternité. France struggled for some time to overcome its historical legacy, but it too eventually established a democracy. Secular moral systems are vested not in god (necessarily), but in reason. "We take these truths to be self-evident…" reads the preamble to the *American Declaration of Independence*. That is, these truths are considered to be obvious, verifiable; *rational*.

Moral precepts embedded in the constitution were stated in universal and secular terms. Following the advice of Montesquieu, Americans adopted a system of legal checks and balances on various branches of government to further limit the discretion of the powerful and increase the likelihood of respect for process. Tantamount to this new system was the language of rights. Though many today assume that the Constitution's author, Thomas Jefferson, was drawing upon John Locke's notions of individual rights, Wills' (2002) insightful exposé reveals the heavy influence upon Jefferson of Scottish humanists like Frances Hutchenson, Thomas Reid, David Hume, and Lord Kames. Unlike Locke, most of these authors believed that human beings have an innate moral nature which informs both their humanity and the societies they construct. Wills' observations enforce the notion that, once freed of archaic moral systems, these philosophers returned to discerning moral principles, in part, by way of intuition. Jefferson had society in mind when he spoke of life, liberty, and the pursuit of happiness. Wills observes that this was nothing private or individual; it meant public happiness. This measurable goal was seen as the test and justification of any government. The *creation story* of the new nation implied that society exists for this natural purpose, which also served as its *metaphysic*. The new *moral code* of a representative democracy based on respect for individual rights became articulated in law.

Thus, the new moral system established the state as the sovereign discerner of moral truth. There would be no higher authority. The state was established as omnipotent, and the final arbiter of good and evil through the court system. Good and evil would be defined as the will of the people in democratic states, though elected political representatives would have decided responsibility in discerning the people's will. Though the major world religions would continue to exist in multiple countries, the state would ultimately allow their existence, form, and means of expression. The state, and not the church, temple, or mosque, would establish a new moral system by describing the conditions under which people are free to practice. Religious freedom would be implemented in the U.S., but priests and clerics would be licensed by the state in order to perform rituals. Still, old moral regimes do not immediately disappear. In time, political leaders from different countries would call upon the same god to help their state be victorious in warfare, each believing that god was on their side.

Although added 2 years later as amendments to the American constitution, a rhetoric of political equality and inalienable individual rights became a part of the U.S. Constitution in the form of a *Bill of Rights*. Seeking to avoid the abuses of power and limitations of freedom in the Old World, certain citizens were granted freedom of religion, free speech, free press, free assembly and the right to petition the government for redress. The Bill of Rights forbade government infringement on the right to bear arms, and persons could not be deprived of life, liberty, or property without due legal process. Other safety measures are described for federal criminal cases, as well as an article clarifying that other rights should not be trampled in the process of protecting those listed in the Bill of Rights. At the time, the idea of entrenching rights into a state constitution was radical, groundbreaking, and prescient. The constitutions of the United States, England, and France became the gold standard and fueled the rise of rights-based constitutions in other parts of the world.

In reality, of course, protection of the handful of civil rights listed in the U.S. Bill of Rights was extended to men of European descent who owned land. Women, slaves, and many racial and ethnic minorities would find little legal protection in the fledgling country. Despite the rhetoric, time and effort is needed to realize and implement the full implications of a new moral system. Though a 20 year limit was placed on the practice of slavery, it would take decades more and a bloody civil war to end the practice. Even today, the U.S. and other nations struggle to shrug off the moral systems of antiquity and realize the full implication of the meaning of equitably protecting the rights of all citizens. And, similar to the concerns of the Vatican regarding the Peace of Westphalia, the respect for rights in the new moral system was not expected to extend beyond its borders.

Human Rights as a Global, Moral System

In the new moral system of the nation-state, rights become embedded in the good will of the state. But who would protect citizens from the state that chooses to be the violator? What would be the defense for those whose rights were violated but not listed in the constitution? Who would protect the rights of persons in a country who are not citizens, or who are citizens of more than one country? These questions were far from esoteric. In some ways, the retreat into nationalism was a maneuver by political elites to coalesce power and prevent other actors from meddling in local affairs. Even with the development of a legal architecture, the danger remained for an abuse of power at the hands of a savvy political elite.

The salience of old tribal identities re-emerged as nation-states asserted ownership of lands filled with the buried bodies of ancient ancestors. Though Enlightenment authors had emphasized equality, their emphasis on reason also spawned a burgeoning quasi-scientific literature that attempted to rationalize existing inequalities of race, class, and culture as based in nature. The sociologist Herbert Spencer, for example, argued that those more intelligent and highly evolved would inevitably find themselves in the top echelons of society; a view quite popular with European and American elites. Charles Darwin would later use Spencer's catch-phrase "the survival of the fittest" to help explain his new theory of evolution.

In the U.S., influential individuals have at times embraced racist, xenophobic, and intolerant perspectives. Despite a constitutional guarantee of civil liberties, the U.S. holds a less-than-stellar record for their protection. Many groups in the U.S. have had to fight for their civil liberties, taking on the very government supposed to protect them. Women were not allowed to vote in all parts of the U.S. until 1920, after 70 years of agitation and against the wishes of then President Woodrow Wilson. African Americans and Hispanics experienced a wide range of both de jure and de facto discriminatory practices which have yet to be fully eliminated. Even white European minorities like the Irish, Italians, and Jews found themselves victims of extreme discrimination on the basis of religious differences, and were denied basic civil rights (Aguirre and Turner 2009).

The events of World War II and its aftermath changed everything. WWII brought to the fore the severe limitations of state sovereignty in guaranteeing universal rights for its citizens. It saw a completely rationalized (Ritzer 2010) yet diabolical institutionalization of genocide on a national level in Germany; a modern "civilized" state, drawing not on values of equality and democracy but of bigotry, intolerance, and racial supremacy. Equally important, it laid bare the logical conclusions of eugenics; a popular movement among many prominent white scientists practicing in Europe and the United States who sought to create a "better" society through genetic engineering and the forced sterilization of humans presumed to be genetically-inferior. Thousands of Americans were sterilized in the name of eugenics before, during, and even after WWII.

New technologies allowed people in WWII to witness the atrocities of the Nazis through photos similar to Figs. 5.1 and 5.2, printed in newspapers, pamphlets, and books. The visceral, aesthetic revulsion to photos of piles of emaciated bodies of concentration camp prisoners reverberated with people around the world. It incited a sense of fear that such atrocities might be repeated and increased the calls for a global bill of rights. "Never again" became the new moral mantra. It set in place a revolution of peoples to protect themselves against governments, creating the conditions for the most universal moral revolution in human history: the human rights revolution.

Fig. 5.1 Bodies of concentration camp prisoners burned alive in their barracks. Schwabmunchen, May 6, 1945. Previously unpublished photo, private collection

Fig. 5.2 Piles of dead concentration camp prisoners. Schwabmunchen, May 6, 1945. Previously unpublished photo, private collection

Legal advocates found a paucity of international law protecting human rights, making it difficult to hold Nazi's accountable for their atrocities during the Nuremberg Trials after the war. Gandhi's peaceful revolution for Indian independence further exposed the brutality and inequality of British colonial rule; a superpower that thought itself to be morally superior and culturally benevolent. This too provided a catalyst to develop a new moral system that transcended the nation state; but one which was more palatable and practical than a universal religion about which no consensus could be achieved.

The stakes to develop preventive mechanisms were also high. The evolution of technological sophistication, so aptly described by Lenski (2005), has always had its perils. Aside from increasing productivity and improving the quality of life, technologies have been developed to increase death and carnage in the face of an enemy. Combined with a leadership committed to the expansion of empire, the consequences of killing technologies have been significant. Between the 13th and 14th centuries, for example, Genghis Khan and his armies killed an estimated forty million people. This large-scale death was enough to actually cool the earth, as acres of land previously cultivated by Kahn's victims returned to forest and absorbed larger amounts of carbon dioxide (Daily Mail 2011). More than two-hundred thousand people died in blasts produced by just two bombs dropped on Hiroshima and Nagasaki, Japan in WWII. More than a hundred thousand were injured. With more countries developing nuclear weaponry, realpolitik could easily result in annihilation on a global scale.

Recognizing the dangers, world leaders decided something had to change. Churchill, Roosevelt, and Stalin were supportive of the idea of forming a United Nations as a way to establish a balance of power. Only at the formative 1945 UN conference in San Francisco did the idea of human rights arise. U.S. consultants succeeded in having human rights mentioned in a draft of the UN's constitution (Schlesinger 2004). U.S. President Roosevelt had earlier popularized the idea of universal rights in his Four Freedoms speech of 1944. He suggested that all peoples of the world should be guaranteed freedom of religion and freedom of speech, as well as freedom from want and freedom from fear. Roosevelt went so far as to suggest a second Bill of Rights be added to the U.S. Constitution to guarantee legal protection of freedom from want and fear. It never materialized.

Institutionalizing Human Rights

The idea of universal rights enjoyed broad appeal with many individuals and organizations from across the world. Morsink (1999) lists the many voices of global citizens, NGO's, religious organizations and others who wrote in support of the creation of an International Bill of Rights. Cuba, Chile, and Panama were among the first countries to draft bills and submit them to the San Francisco conference. The notion was so popular that a UN Human Rights Commission was established at the outset, with Eleanor Roosevelt serving as Chair. The drafting process was deliberately inclusive and open as a religiously, politically, and ethnically diverse drafting committee was organized. That agreement on a universal moral statement of 30 articles would be achieved, let alone accepted by the UN General Assembly on December 10, 1948, is a testament to its applicability, relevance, and readiness of the world at that time to embrace a new moral statement universal in its intent.

The impact of this new moral ideal was immediate in the U.S. Hispanic, Asian American, and African American soldiers returned from service in World War II to encounter ongoing racism and discrimination. Fueled with a new understanding of rights and the experience of fighting to protect the human rights of others, social movements were launched in the name of equal rights. Jim Crow segregation in the South ended as a result of the Civil Rights movement. Hispanics successfully overturned de jure discriminatory practices in Texas through a U.S. Supreme Court challenge. Similar rights-based movements challenged child labor practices, sexism, ageism, and the discriminatory treatment of people with disabilities, as well as gays, lesbians, bisexuals, and transgendered people.

The explosion of interest and work in human rights around the globe since WWII has been substantial. Foremost among these has been the UN's construction of an International Bill of Rights, adding two binding covenants; the International Covenant on Civil and Political Rights (ICCPR) and the International Covenant on Economic, Social and Cultural Rights (ICESCR), to the UDHR. Nine additional major human rights declarations have also been released for ratification, and a permanent International Criminal Court was established in 2002. Hundreds of international non-government organizations (INGOs) like *Amnesty International*, *Doctors Without Borders* and *Sociologists Without Borders* have formed to work for the protection and advancement of human rights, along with thousands of domestic non-government organizations (NGOs). In the U.S., the *American Civil Liberties Union* (ACLU) opened a human rights office in 2003, while the American Association for the Advancement of Science (AAAS) organized an interdisciplinary Science and Human Rights Coalition to further the human right of people to benefit from the advancements of science. Individual academic disciplines are likewise being influenced by the new moral code, creating policies respecting human rights and subsections dedicated to the topic. Frezzo (2011) details the growing influence of human rights within my own discipline of Sociology, while Brunsma et al. (2013) illustrate the profound impact of a human rights paradigm in every major sub-discipline of Sociology.

More than 50 state constitutions today make reference to human rights. Newer state constitutions such as Kosovo's have even included deferential statements to human rights by declaring, "Ratified international agreements and legally binding norms of international law have superiority over the laws of the Republic of Kosovo" (Article 19.2). Domestic and international human rights instruments continue to be enacted. A database created by Elliott (2011) contains a total of 779 distinct human rights instruments; the vast majority created after WWII, but some enacted as early as 1863. Regional human rights treaties have likewise been an important part of the trend to establish an international moral framework, as their creation required international cooperation. Just prior to the formation of the UN, representatives from states in the Western hemisphere met in April 1948 in Bogotá, Columbia to adopt the world's first general human rights document: The American Declaration of the Rights and Duties of Man (ADRDM). This document, signed by the U.S., was an inspiration for the UDHR which was to follow. The Council of Europe produced The Convention for the Protection of Human Rights and Fundamental Freedoms (CPHRFF), opened for signature in 1950. The African Union implemented the African Charter on Human and Peoples' Rights (ACHPR) in 1986 while the Arab Charter on Human Rights, produced by the League of Arab States, came into effect in 2008. Of interest is the moral tone of the preamble to each of these documents, seeking the recognition and establishment of justice, "brotherhood," and equality.

The reverberations of the movement continue to be felt across the globe. Foreign television and radio programs beamed into the former Eastern Bloc made residents aware of the huge disparity in freedoms and quality of life in countries outside of the bloc, contributing to the implosion of the system. The new Czech Republic was formed though the Velvet Revolution, where more than a half-million citizens publically and non-violently expressed their desire for a new regime that would do better at respecting their rights and providing them with opportunities. International pressure by human rights organizations were a part of the catalyst to dismantle Apartheid in South Africa and to free political prisoner Nelson Mandela. Other attempts to usher in democracy and greater freedoms—from Tienmenn Square to the Arab Spring protests in Egypt, Bahrain, and elsewhere—have in part or in whole been fueled by a growing understanding and embracing of human rights principles. Because of their widespread popularity and their likely ontological grounding in the human condition (Walsh 2012), it is not disingenuous to refer to the growth of human rights as an *indigenous global moral movement*.

Equally telling is the manner in which political and religious global moral authorities are either voicing respect for human rights or having the moral legitimacy of their actions evaluated by human rights standards. The 2013 election of Pope Francis is significant, as he has indicated his desire to shift emphasis in Catholicism from dogma to tolerance, social justice, and humanitarianism. More surprising, perhaps, is the declaration of the Dalai Lama, leader of the world's Buddhist faith, in his recent book *Beyond Religion* (Lama and Norman 2012). He states that, though the world's major religions can promote inner values of love, compassion, and tolerance, grounding ethics in religion is no longer adequate. He suggests that the time has come to think about spirituality and ethics beyond religion altogether. Human rights specialist Donnelly (1998) has argued that human rights have become the new standard of civilization. Perhaps another indication is to follow the money. A recent study found that Americans are giving less money to religious organizations but are giving more overall to other charities (Fottrell 2013).

Taken together, these trends and examples point to the emergence of a global consciousness and to human rights as a global moral system. The accepted *creation story* of human beings differs across the world, but the integrity of the moral system no longer depends on uniformity. Indeed, human rights themes resonate equally with persons of faith, persons of different faiths, and persons who embrace no faith. The *metaphysic* is the notion to live and let live, and to share some resources to empower ourselves and others for individual and collective development. The minimal *moral code* is expressed in the thirty articles of the Universal Declaration of Human Rights, though some would add the additional Declarations to the list.

References

Aguirre, A., Jr., & Turner, J. (2009). *American ethnicity: The dynamics and consequences of discrimination* (6th ed.). Boston, MA: McGraw-Hill.

Brunsma, D., Smith, K. E., & Gran, B. K. (Eds.). (2013). *Handbook of the sociology of human rights*. Boulder, CO: Paradigm.

Daily Mail. (2011, January 25). Genghis Khan the GREEN. *Daily Mail Online*. http://www.dailymail.co.uk/sciencetech/article-1350272/Genghis-Khan-killed-people-forests-grew-carbon-levels-dropped.html. Accessed 28 December 2013.

Donnelly, J. (1998). Human rights: A new standard of civilization? *International Affairs, 74*(1), 1–23.

Elliott, M. (2011). The institutional expansion of human rights, 1863–2003: A comprehensive dataset of international instruments. *Journal of Peace Research, 48*, 537–546.

Fottrell, Q. (2013, June 22). Americans are giving less money to god. *MarketWatch*. http://www.marketwatch.com/story/americans-are-giving-less-money-to-god-2013-06-20. Accessed 29 December 2013.

Frezzo, M. (2011). Sociology and human rights in the post-development era. *Sociology Compass, 5*(3), 203–214.

Goodman, L. (2003). *Islamic humanism*. London: Oxford University Press.

Holt, J. (2008). *Magna Carta*. New York: Cambridge University Press.

Ishay, M. (2008). *The history of human rights*. Berkeley: University of California Press.

Kraemer, J. (1992). *Humanism in the renaissance of islam*. Leiden, Netherlands: Brill.

Lama, D. H. H. and Norman, A. (2012). *Beyond Religion: Ethics for a Whole World*. New York: Mariner.

Lapidus, I. (1992). The golden age: The political concepts of islam. *Annals of the American Academy of Political and Social Science, 524*, 13–25.

Lenski, G. (2005). *Ecological-Evolutionary Theory*. Boulder, CO: Paradigm.

Morsink, J. (1999). *The universal declaration of human rights: Origins*. Philadelphia: University of Pennsylvania Press.

Pagden, A. (1982). *The fall of natural man*. London: Cambridge University Press.

Ritzer, G. (2010). *The McDonaldization of society 6*. Thousand Oaks, CA: Sage.

Schlesinger, S. (2004). *Act of creation*. New York: Basic Books.

Walsh, Vincent. (2012). Universal moral grammar: An ontological grounding for human rights. *Societies Without Borders, 7*(1), 74–99.

Wills, G. (2002). *Inventing America*. New York: Mariner.

Chapter 6
Convergence and Frontiers

In this brief monograph I have tried to provide an outline of a theory of morality and illustrate its potential to explain moral paradigmatic shifts. In revising key concepts from Durkheim, I chose to shift focus from religion per se to underlying systems of morality. I also introduced the concept of the nonmoral to signify parts of the world that exist outside of the worldview shared by members of a society. Because they exist outside the moral system, people and things not assigned a moral status can be treated in cruel or inhumane ways.

I have purposely avoided the use of religious terms and metaphors, even in a redefined sociological sense, in an effort to clarify biological and social processes that collectively contribute to the development, maintenance, and evolution of moral systems. I also intentionally selected a definition of religion that has popular appeal and has the ability to more carefully distinguish religious versus nonreligious phenomena. Doing so, I trust, helps to reveal the more intentional ways in which religious beliefs and practices emerged as societies increased in size and complexity. Focusing on morality also opens the possibility to better understand the small but persistent growth of nonbelief in modern societies, and illustrates that morals have, and do, exist outside the purview of religion. The analysis suggests that it is morality, and not necessarily religion, which emanates from the human condition. At the same time, religions have the potential to draw attention to and increase respect for innate tendencies which people so readily equate with morality.

A review of recent research into the "moral" behavior of non-human primates, as well as young children and adults, revealed fascinating behaviors that are near-universal and replicable. I use quotation marks to imply that the moral label is an attribution of a state of being. What we actually observe are consistent emotional responses to social stimuli. These responses are either pleasurable or uncomfortable, but assigning value or preference to such conditions is a separate, socially constructive process. Many would no doubt prefer the utilitarian vision

© The Author(s) 2015
B.K. Friesen, *Moral Systems and the Evolution of Human Rights*,
SpringerBriefs in Sociology, DOI 10.1007/978-94-017-9551-7_6

of constructing a moral system which maximizes positive emotional states in the greatest number of people. Yet emotional states are remarkably unstable and rather temporal. Human needs, wants, and our willingness to exchange certain amounts of personal autonomy for the privilege of living in community or having more important needs met—are far more durable than an emotional state at any particular moment in time. Any moral philosophy will need to balance the pleasure induced in certain emotional states with other important concerns.

Modernity has witnessed the reorganization of human groups into a social form known as the nation-state. Though in part a backlash to the meddling of outsiders in local affairs, the formation of nation states sewed the seeds of a larger, more inclusive secular moral system. The global challenges of WWII, in turn, exposed the inherent shortcomings of such. By focusing on all people of the world, the authors of the Universal Declaration of Human Rights created an ethic more abstract than others and yet with intuitive appeal.

To be sure, the moral system of human rights has some decided advantages over those that have come before. For the first time in human history, humans have devised a way to live together which involves no "Them." All members of the human species are included. Human beings have an affinity towards developing a tribal identity, but human history has shown just how pliable such identities are. Illustrative of this is the strong sense of patriotism among members of nation-states with populations numbering in the hundreds of millions. If the notion of homo-sapiens-as-tribe is realized, the moral system of human rights could potentially decrease violent intergroup conflicts and warfare. Similar to the more intuitive moral systems of hunting and gathering societies, membership in the human rights system is ascriptive. Unlike major world religions, no conversion or pledging is needed. Ascetic rituals, sacrifices, giving, or homage not required in order to maintain membership. The one thing required is to respect the rights of others; to live and let live. Human rights principles capitalize on the interdependence of human beings by qualifying the ways in which people should treat each other so as to realize optimum outcomes.

Yet if the theory of the evolution of moral systems has any merit, there is every reason to believe that moral evolution will continue. Societies continue to change. Human beings continue to evolve. Counter-movements can certainly occur in which older moral systems regain momentum. Conceptual systems too have a way of expanding. I thus conclude the discussion of human rights with two plausible future scenarios, and leave it to you to decide which is most prescient. Perhaps you can think of a third.

Scenario 1: Human Rights as Myth and Ceremony

Though the human rights initiatives mentioned above are observable, counter-forces which seek to disable human rights efforts are also real. These forces often originate among those who see themselves being disadvantaged by the human rights system; usually the most powerful. The failed experience with the League of Nations, a forerunner to the United Nations, is telling. In an effort to inhibit the possibility of another widespread war, global leaders created the League of Nations after WWI. Built on the principle of equality, all member nations received a single vote in the fledgling organization. Leaders of the more powerful nations soon found the mechanisms of the League wanting, however. It required them to defer to decisions made by a body apart from the sovereign nation-state; one in which the poorest and weakest nations of the world had as much political clout as the highly-industrialized nations. Many found the situation impalpable. As there were no mechanisms in place to hold countries accountable for failing to comply with decisions made by the League, the organization soon dissipated, and WWII occurred not long after. Learning from the past, architects of the present United Nations created the Security Council and other apparatuses to give additional powers and privileged status to first-world nations.

Membership in the United Nations is largely voluntary, as is the option of signing and ratifying human rights treaties. Enforcement mechanisms are weak for those that fail to live up to commitments, especially for first world actors. This is likely intentional as many global leaders resist being held accountable. Morsink (1999) details a telling moment regarding the inclusion of the following phrase in the preamble to the UDHR: *Whereas it is essential, if man is not to be compelled to have recourse, as a last resort, to rebellion against tyranny and oppression, that human rights should be protected by the rule of law.* While members of the committee recognized that tyranny and oppression should be met with resistance, few wanted to legitimate rebellion of any kind. Even after several re-wordings, the item still was one that received a lower amount of support.

For many nations, signing human rights instruments still appears to be little more than myth and ceremony; a phrase used by Meyer and Rowan (1977) to describe a situation where an institutional statement or practice is implemented in an organization to appear that they have addressed a situation. In reality, however, little if any change in real behavior occurs. The International Criminal Court (ICC) was established in 2002 as a way of holding global leaders accountable for violating human rights standards. A full forty-one nations have refused to endorse the ICC, including the United States. Cole (2012) found that compliance with human rights instruments is greater when it is accompanied by optional monitoring and enforcement mechanisms, but leaders of the Global South are frustrated with ways in which leaders of first-world nations continue to *game the system*; with human rights monitoring processes or other issues. In a show of solidarity, leaders of 132 nations walked out of the 2013 climate talks in Warsaw to protest the refusal of first-world nation leaders to engage in a dialogue regarding climate change recompense (Vidal 2013).

Realpolitik—a desire to get one's way regardless of the issues—often overshadows a concern for human rights, but there are others for whom resistance against human rights standards takes on a moral tone. There are those in powerful positions that resent the paradigmatic moral shift to human rights and cling tenaciously to a belief in the righteousness of state sovereignty. Cox (2008) details how many conservative Republicans, particularly in the southeastern U.S., have persistently lobbied to defund the UN and have found ways to eviscerate any mechanisms of holding the U.S. accountable for failing to upholding human rights standards at home. Cox suggests that these initiatives are in part motivated out of fear that current voting or labor policies which adversely affect the plight of minorities might be re-examined, but for others, the notion of the United States deferring to any higher authority is morally repugnant.

The disregard for human rights compliance by powerful nations illustrates that the human rights moral revolution is anything but inevitable. The current political turmoil in the U.S. is indicative of the confusion wrought by shifts in the moral paradigm, with politicians largely split between an attempt to inhibit change and those who see initiatives to integrate a greater diversity of peoples into society as a no-brainer. Though the U.S. played a lead role in establishing the UN and creating the UDHR, the political power of those morally committed to maintaining state sovereignty in spite of global commitments has gained momentum. The U.S. has largely ceased to sign human instruments, and stipulates so many conditions when it does that it renders accountability virtually impossible. As with the League of Nations, noncompliance by powerful nations can also establish powerful precedents in ignoring human rights principles and mechanisms. Blau et al. (2008) offer an insightful analysis detailing the U.S.' poor record of domestic human rights; lagging behind virtually every other modern nation in quality of life indicators for its citizens, including housing, health, worker rights, indigenous peoples rights, cultural rights, and more.

The U.S.' dissention-by-example may set a precedent for leaders of other nations to do the same. In 2012, Russia succeeded in gaining the approval of the UN's Human Rights Council for a policy endorsing the "traditional values of humankind;" code for endorsing anti-homosexual policies (Reid 2012). In 2013, the United Kingdom's initiative for curricular reform in its public schools came under heavy criticism for emphasizing citizenship over human rights education; a violation of the *UN Convention on the Rights of the Child* (McGuffin 2013). The U.S. Supreme Court essentially gutted the Voting Rights Act in 2014; a cornerstone piece of legislation protecting the right to vote.

Aside from the realpolitik interests and moral repudiation of human rights claims, the cognitive work needed for ordinary people to fully comprehend the implications of human rights can be problematic. Moral systems become increasingly abstract as the group to which they are applied grows ever larger. Some aspects of human rights are indeed intuitive—an emphasis on fairness, empathy, and respect. Other aspects require a mental transcending of categories of difference long used by social groups to categorize and devalue, such as sex, race, religion, nationality, and language. Blattberg (2009) illustrates this in an essay entitled, *The Ironic Tragedy of Human Rights*. He contentiously argues that human rights have created the conditions that make mass murder more, rather than less, likely. He asks the reader to consider their own visceral response to two pieces of information. The first is a simple declaration that the rights of six million human beings were violated by the Nazis in WWII. The second is a vivid and personal retelling of an experience of torture at the hands of the Nazis by a concentration camp survivor. The prisoner recounts in vivid detail how his hands, tied behind his back, were lifted by a hook and chain connected to a pulley in the ceiling. Recounting the pain and his initial physical resistance, he describes the crackling and splintering in his shoulders as the balls sprang from their sockets, while his clothing was shredded by repeated blows from a horsewhip.

By asking us to consider which of the two pieces of information has the greater impact, Blattberg reminds us that our primal emotions of empathy are stimulated at the personal, not the abstract level. They are visceral. Because human rights are largely enshrined in abstract documents created by distant professionals with whom most people never come in contact, the idea of human rights principles may not readily resonate. Blattberg might disagree, but it seems to follow that human rights *can* be made meaningful as long as they continue to be grounded in individual human experience. There is no guarantee that this will be accomplished and, thus, no guarantee that the human rights revolution will be sustained. Indeed, part of the attraction to other increasingly popular political philosophies like libertarianism, anarchism, or the tribalisms of the past, could be a reversion back to more intuitive political arrangements and their incumbent moral systems.

Scenario 2: Further Expansion of Rights

On the other hand, it is possible that the global trend to embrace and institutionalize human rights described in the previous chapter may continue. Lenski (2005: 62) points out that the number of societies in the world has decreased 99 % in the past 10,000 years. Along with a consolidation of territory and a coalescing of power, moral systems have likewise merged and converged. If an emphasis on human rights continues, government leaders will be compelled to respect human rights commitments and fully ratify the range of international human rights instruments. Monitoring and evaluative mechanisms will increase in importance, and real resources will be dedicated to improving human rights conditions both domestically and internationally. Concern for human rights could expand from simple civil and political rights to the more complex cultural, social, and economic rights. More countries would likely structure themselves in a manner similar to Western European democracies where government programs provide a wide range of services and opportunities for their citizens as such programs are far cheaper and more effective than piecemeal services offered via the market. In many parts of the world, embracing of human rights would involve a fundamental redefinition of society and government. Ultimately, the elimination of absolute poverty would be expected and a more sophisticated global citizenry would emerge as education and economic opportunities increase. Far more than changes in international law or UN declarations, the genuine power of human rights as a moral system resides in the ability of a moral system to validate the feelings of people at the grassroots level that it is right and good to demand to be treated with dignity and respect.

It is very possible that a discourse related to the clarification and reinterpretation of rights will continue as societies change and human beings continue to evolve. Though presented as universal and unchanging, it is not difficult to see that some of the thirty articles in the UDHR presuppose current conditions as they are. Article 23 states that everyone has the right to work and to free choice of employment. These rights would cease to be a concern in a future society that manages to establish a guaranteed annual income for all citizens, debated even now (http://www.incomesecurityforall.org/). In such a scenario, work could become optional. Article 16 states that men and women of full age have the right to marry and found a family, but there is already significant pressure to extend those rights to gay, lesbian, bisexual, and transgendered individuals.

The most immediate consequence of this scenario is the expansion of rights. Nine major human rights instruments and two covenants, articulating new human rights for various groups, have been created by the UN since the ratification of the UDHR. Others can be anticipated. Equally plausible is the extension of rights to non-human entities. New Zealand, Spain, and other countries have implemented various forms of rights protections for apes as advocated by Cavalieri and Singer (1994). Many established groups, including the *American Society for the Prevention of Cruelty to Animals*, lobby for additional laws protecting the *rights* of animals. More abstractly, lobbying continues to advocate for the rights of mother nature (http://therightsofnature.org/). Lacking legal identity, some have taken the reverse tact of attempting to define non-persons as persons, therefore entitling these entities to the same rights under law as human persons. The U.S. Supreme Court established corporate personhood as early as 1888. In New Zealand, the indigenous Maori people successfully lobbied its government into granting personhood to the Whanganui River, granting it legal rights in 2013.

New rights-based challenges in the form of human hybrids will present themselves in the next 30–40 years. People will have to decide if some variant of a *cyborg*—part human, part machine—should be accorded human rights. It may sound far-fetched, but a certain degree of humanlike-consciousness has already been achieved in some robots as envisioned in *Bicentennial Man, I Robot*, or even the old *Terminator* series of movies. I would guess the number of people who support awarding R2D2 of *Star Wars* human rights would outnumber those who would not, its fictional status notwithstanding.

Human clones may soon appear with a host of rights issues all their own, and perhaps humans who have had bodily organs replaced with the organs of animals might present questions regarding the definition of what it means to be human and thus accorded certain human rights. Pushing this just a little farther, we are rapidly mapping the genomes of dozens of species and finding how to alter gene expression. If we find we can manipulate genes to allow for more inter-species breeding, a whole new range of part-human life-forms could emerge. Would minotaurs or centaurs be deserving of human rights protections?

Respect for human rights seems in many ways to solve some of the moral dilemmas of our current reality, but they too are predicated on essentialist assumptions that the human condition is unchanging. Such an assumption fails to incorporate substantial evidence that human beings continue to evolve. White (2013) notes the changes that have occurred in humans within the last 50,000 years alone. As global migration commenced, the skin lightened of those who settled in northern climes; an adaptive mechanism improving vitamin D synthesis in the sun-scarce north. Further adaptations involved straight hair in Asians, blue eyes in Europeans, the shorter stature of "Pygmy" populations in tropical forests, and genetic adaptations of Andean, Tibetan, and Ethiopian high-altitude environments that made breathing easier. We've changed from a nomadic to a sedentary species, altering our immune systems and metabolism. Those living in dairy-consuming societies have developed a lactose tolerance. Today's increasing global mobility further stirs up the gene pool and challenges human organisms to adapt to new diseases and insects. Indeed, the fact-paced social changes experienced in the last 500 years are placing ever-increasing pressure on the human species to evolve at a faster pace. This includes the potentially game-changing developments of antibiotics, vaccines, mass-produced food, fertility drugs, genetically modified organisms in the food supply, climate change, and more. Any truly inclusive moral system will have to be highly adaptive and flexible to allow for future social and biological evolution. Therein lies the conundrum. To increase their importance, moral systems have always been tied to a belief in something essential and unchanging. Is it possible that a dynamic moral system might yet evolve?

Any moral system predicated on a static notion of human nature is destined to become antiquated at some point. Certainly, instinctual biases towards fairness, sociability, reciprocity, and empathy have been demonstrated to be a core component of the human condition. But if we evolve a different set of emotional responses to social stimuli over time, will that make us less human? I hardly think so, though punitive systems of social control currently imply that to be the case with some narcissists, people with autism, psychopaths, or others who display different emotional responses to certain social stimuli than what is considered to be "normal." What percentage of the population has to exhibit different emotional responses before the moral system is modified to include, account for, or respond to those of us with relatively unique internal compositions?

Human Rights: An Applied Sociology

A final word about the here and now. If I blur the lines between describing what *is* and what *ought* to be here, know that I am remaining faithful to the ontological roots of my discipline (Friesen 2012). The Enlightenment gave birth to the discipline of Sociology, aspiring to make use of scientific knowledge to design "better" systems of social organization. I embrace the Sociological tradition of defining *better* social systems as those which produce more happiness for more people rather than less, yet not at the expense of the increasing unhappiness or discomfort of a few. At this moment in our evolutionary history, human beings are faced with a choice of embracing and refining the burgeoning global system of human rights or rejecting it. Though fraught with challenges, it appears that the human rights system of morality is "better" suited for current-day realities than other alternatives. Any attempt to create a global religion at this point will produce more bloodshed than the world has yet to see, as resistance will come both from members of other religions *and* the growing percentage of non-religious persons. Utopian movements like anarchism or libertarianism would ultimately create vulnerabilities due to a power imbalance that larger, more powerful coalitions of human beings would be only too happy to exploit. Such has been the history of humankind.

Human rights honors existing political realities while encouraging initiatives that attempt to produce greater happiness. An international institutional architecture built on respect for human rights has already been established. A respect for human rights requires none to relinquish their religious faith. Indeed, faith often enhances one's commitment to human rights. Done correctly, a human rights morality embeds a global ethic within human experience and honors our vulnerabilities, our needs, and even our dreams. Intellectuals will continue to make problematic the ontological and epistemological foundations of human rights, but a moral system that offers enough of an excuse to motivate people to respect the needs and vulnerabilities of others while having the same reciprocated is a vast improvement over what has thus far been achieved.

This is because, ultimately, it is human vulnerabilities and needs that are *real*. They may change over time, but much has remained constant for at least the past several millennia. Human beings; our natural tendencies, and our needs for things like connection, equality, and development: those things are real. Society—and morality—is but a social construction. This awareness should be emancipatory. Our need for society and morality grows out of recognition of our interdependence for mutual need satisfaction. The task at hand is to design a social arrangement and an incumbent moral system that fully honors human vulnerability and needs while remaining dynamic enough to account for human diversity and our continuing biological and social evolution. As I mentioned earlier, the last 12,000 years of human society-building has been a history of deciding whose needs will be met first, most, and at what cost to others. We now have the conceptual, moral, and technological capacity to extend the focus to all of humanity. Noble is the person who heeds Shulamith Koenig's[1] call to make human rights *a way of life*.

---

[1] Shulamith Koenig is one of five Americans to have been awarded the UN Prize in the Field of Human Rights, along with Eleanor Roosevelt, Martin Luther King Jr., Jimmy Carter, and James Grant. See http://www.pdhre.org/people/shulabio.html.

References

Blattberg, C. (2009). The ironic tragedy of human rights. In *Patriotic elaborations: Essays in practical philosophy*. Montreal: McGill-Queen's University Press.

Blau, J., Brunsma, D., Moncada, A., & Zimmer, C. (Eds.). (2008). *The leading rogue state: The U.S. and human rights*. Boulder, CO: Paradigm.

Cavalieri, P., & Singer, P. (1994). *The great ape project: Equality beyond humanity*. New York: St. Martin's.

Cole, W. (2012). Human rights as myth and ceremony? Reevaluating the effectiveness of human rights treaties, 1981 to 2007. *American Journal of Sociology, 117*(4), 1131–1171.

Cox, L. (2008). A movement for human rights in the United States: reasons for hope. *Columbia Human Rights Law Review, 40*, 135–137.

Friesen, B. K. (2012). Science: Acknowledging context. *Societies Without Borders, 7*(2), 238–241. http://societieswithoutborders.files.wordpress.com/2012/08/symposium20121.pdf.

Lenski, G. (2005). *Ecological-evolutionary theory*. Boulder, CO: Paradigm.

McGuffin, P. (2013, February 8). Human rights NGOs hit out at a new curriculum folly. *Morning Star Online*. http://www.morningstaronline.co.uk/news/content/view/full/129243. Accessed 9 February 2013.

Meyer, J., & Rowan, B. (1977). Institutional organizations: Formal structure as myth and ceremony. *American Journal of Sociology, 83*, 340–363.

Morsink, J. (1999). *The universal declaration of human rights: Origins, drafting, and intent*. Philadelphia: University of Pennsylvania Press.

Reid, G. (2012, October 17). 'Traditional values' code for human rights abuse? CNN Online. http://globalpublicsquare.blogs.cnn.com/2012/10/17/traditional-values-code-for-human-rights-abuse/. Accessed 30 December 2013.

Vidal, J. (2013, November 20). Poor countries walk out of UN climate change talks as compensation row rumbles on. *The Guardian*. http://www.theguardian.com/global-development/2013/nov/20/climate-talks-walk-out-compensation-un-warsaw. Accessed 3 December 2013.

White, M. (2013, November 17). Are we still evolving? *Pacific Standard*. www.psmag.com/science/still-evolving-69121. Accessed 30 December 2013.

Index

© The Author(s) 2015
B.K. Friesen, *Moral Systems and the Evolution of Human Rights*,
SpringerBriefs in Sociology, DOI 10.1007/978-94-017-9551-7

CPSIA information can be obtained at www.ICGtesting.com
Printed in the USA
BVOW08s1806160115

383682BV00005B/22/P